DOUGLAS SBD DAUNTLESS
PILOT'S FLIGHT OPERATING

INSTRUCTIONS

Navy Model
SBD-6
Airplanes

NOTICE. — This document contains information affecting the national defense of the United States within the meaning of the Espionage Act, 50 U.S.C., 31 and 32, as amended. Its transmission or the revelation of its contents in any manner to an unauthorized person is prohibited by law.

PILOT'S FLIGHT OPERATING INSTRUCTIONS

Navy Model
SBD-6
Airplanes

Published by authority of
The Chief of The Bureau of Aeronautics

THIS PUBLICATION MAY BE USED BY PERSONNEL RENDERING
SERVICE TO THE UNITED STATES OR ITS ALLIES

Navy Regulations, Article 75½, contains the following paragraphs relating to the handling of restricted matter:

(b) *Restricted* matter may be disclosed to persons of discretion in the Government service when it appears to be in the public interest.

(c) *Restricted* matter may be disclosed, under special circumstances, to persons not in the Government service when it appears to be in the public interest.

The Bureau of Aeronautics Circular Letter No. 12-43 further states:

Therefore, it is requested that all naval activities check their own local regulations and procedures to make sure that handbooks, service instructions, and other *restricted* technical publications are actually being made available to both civilian and enlisted personnel who have use for them.

Paragraph 5 (d) of Army Regulation 380-5 relative to handling of *restricted* printed matter is quoted below:

(d) Dissemination of restricted matter.—The information contained in restricted documents and the essential characteristics of restricted material may be given to *any person known to be in the service of the United States and to persons of undoubted loyalty and discretion who are co-operating in Government work*, but will not be communicated to the public or to the press except by authorized military public relations agencies.

These instructions permit the issue of *restricted* publications to civilian contract and other accredited schools engaged in training personnel for Government work, to civilian concerns contracting for overhaul and repair of aircraft or aircraft accessories, and to similar commercial organizations.

LIST OF REVISED PAGES ISSUED

NOTE.—A heavy black vertical line to the left of the text on revised pages indicates the extent of the revision. This line is omitted where more than 50 percent of the page is involved.

ADDITIONAL COPIES OF THIS PUBLICATION MAY BE OBTAINED AS FOLLOWS:

AAF ACTIVITIES.—Submit requisions to the Commanding General, Fairfield Air Service Command, Patterson Field, Fairfield, Ohio, Attention: Publications Distribution Branch, in acordance with AAF Regulation No. 5-9. Also, for details of Technical Order distribution, see T.O. No. 00-25-3.

NAVY ACTIVITIES.—Submit requests to the Chief, Bureau of Aeronautics, Navy Department, Washington, D. C.

THIS PAGE INTENTIONALLY LEFT BLANK.

Figure 1—Final Views of SBD-6 Airplane

FOREWORD

This handbook has been compiled to acquaint operating personnel assigned to the Douglas Dive Bomber, Model SBD-6, with its general characteristics, equipment, and method of operation. The contents of this manual should be thoroughly studied before the pilot's first flight.

THIS PAGE INTENTIONALLY LEFT BLANK.

CONTENTS

Section I

COCKPIT ARRANGEMENT AND CONTROLS

Section II
POWER PLANT

Section III
OPERATION CHARTS AND DATA

Section IV
AIRPLANE CHARACTERISTICS

Index

ILLUSTRATIONS

THIS PAGE INTENTIONALLY LEFT BLANK.

INTRODUCTION

In general, the Douglas Dive Bomber, Model SBD-6, is operated in the conventional manner and performs all ground and flight maneuvers with the normal characteristics of its type. The Model SBD-6 (Type VSB) is a single-engined, two-seated, fully cantilevered, low-wing monoplane. As a landplane, it will take off from the ground; or it will take off from the deck of a carrier with or without the aid of a catapult. The airplane will land on an ordinary landing field, or on a carrier deck with the aid of an arresting gear. This model is designed to complete the missions usually assigned to dive bombers, smoke layers, and scout airplanes.

All information concerning the proper operation of this airplane, together with its salient characteristics, is given in this handbook.

THIS PAGE INTENTIONALLY LEFT BLANK.

SECTION I
COCKPIT ARRANGEMENT AND CONTROLS

1. GENERAL.

The Model SBD-6 Dive Bomber is designed to be flown from the pilot's cockpit. However, auxiliary controls in the rear compartment permit the airplane to be flown by the gunner. The controls are divided into four sections: Flight Controls; Power Plant Controls; Auxiliary Controls; and Useful Load Installation Controls. For the identification and arrangement of the various controls, refer to the illustrations included in the following pages.

2. FLIGHT CONTROLS.

The pilot and gunner are provided with tandem stick-and-pedal-type controls which are operated in the conventional manner. Controls for the aileron trim tab, elevator trim tabs, and rudder trim tab are directly to the left of the pilot's seat. Individual tab movement is registered in degrees on an indicator beside each tab control. The control quadrant for the landing and diving flaps is directly to the right of the pilot's seat. An indicator to the right of the control quadrant indicates the position of the flaps. Control surfaces can be locked in neutral when the airplane is parked or moored.

a. CONTROL STICK (Figure 3).

(1) A conventional-type control stick is installed in the pilot's cockpit and in the gunner's compartment. The gunner's control stick can be easily removed and stowed in the clips mounted on the left wall of the compartment (Figure 31, Item 11).

(2) The control stick provides lateral and longitudinal control of the airplane by means of the ailerons and elevators. Side motion of the control stick operates the ailerons; fore and aft movement operates the elevators.

(3) Trigger and bomb release switches are incorporated in the handle of the pilot's control stick. The trigger switch fires the fixed guns and is on the forward side of the handle; the bomb release switch is a button on top of the handle.

b. RUDDER PEDALS (Figure 2, Item 10). —
Conventional-type rudder pedals are installed in the pilot's cockpit and in the gunner's compartment. The rudder pedals provide directional control of the airplane by means of the rudder. Actuation of either rudder pedal operates the rudder. For adjustment of the rudder pedals, see Paragraph 4.1.

c. TRIM TAB CONTROLS (Figure 4).

(1) The aileron trim tab control wheel (Figure 6, Item 8) provides lateral trim of the airplane by means of a tab incorporated in the left aileron. Turn the control wheel to the right or left to obtain lateral trim.

NOTE

The direction of movement of the trim tab controls corresponds to the resultant control of the airplane.

(2) The elevator trim tab control wheel (Figure 6, Item 9) provides longitudinal trim of the airplane by the action of a tab in each elevator. Rotate the control wheel fore or aft to obtain longitudinal control of the airplane.

(3) The rudder trim tab control dial (Figure 6, Item 6) provides directional trim of the airplane by means of a tab incorporated in the rudder. Turn the control dial to the right or left to obtain the desired directional trim.

d. LANDING FLAP CONTROL (Figure 7, Item 4).

(1) The landing flap selector lever (black knob) controls the operation of the split-edge type landing flaps. The landing flaps increase the gliding angle of the airplane for landing and decrease the stalling speed; they are also used to shorten the take-off distance.

CAUTION

Do not lower the landing flaps at an indicated air speed exceeding 110 knots and do not exceed 125 knots after they are lowered. (Refer to the note following Paragraph 1. in Section IV.)

(2) To lower the landing flaps, move the selector lever to the "DOWN" position and depress the engine pump control handle (Figure 7, Item 6). Normally, three seconds are required for this operation.

CAUTION

Before the landing flaps are operated, the diving flap selector lever must be in the

1	Compass	8	Brake Pedals	14	Carburetor Air Control
2	Windshield Heat Control	9	Oil Cooler Scoop Control	15	Starter Control
3	Parking Brake Control	10	Rudder Pedals	16	Bomb Release Button
4	Cowl Flap Control	11	Landing Gear Position Indicator	17	Brake Pedal Adjustment
5	Ignition Switch	12	Fixed Gun Sight	18	Cockpit Ventilator Control
6	Throttle Control	13	Automatic Pilot Control	19	Control Stick Handle
7	Carburetor Air Filter Control			20	Rudder Pedal Adjustment

Figure 2—Pilot's Cockpit—Front

"CLOSED" position, and the landing gear selector lever must be either full "UP" or full "DOWN."

(3) **To partially lower** the landing flaps, move the selector lever to the "DOWN" position and operate the hydraulic hand pump (Figure 5, Item 4). When the flap indicator registers the desired position, return the selector lever to a neutral position (midway between "UP" and "DOWN").

(4) **To raise** the landing flaps move the selector lever to the "UP" position and depress the engine pump control handle (Figure 7, Item 6). Normally, three seconds are required for this operation.

NOTE

In case of engine pump failure, use the hydraulic hand pump (Figure 5, Item 4). Twenty strokes will result in 38 degrees of flap movement.

(5) Normally, the landing flap selector lever remains in the "UP" position when the flaps are raised. However, in case of hydraulic line failure, place the selector lever in a neutral position to prevent the fluid in the reservoir from being pumped overboard.

CAUTION

Place the landing flap selector lever in the "UP" position when the airplane is parked.

(6) When the landing flaps are in the "DOWN" position and it is necessary to flatten (or lengthen) the glide of the airplane in an emergency, place the selector lever in the "UP" position. When the engine is not operating, lower the flaps when it is certain that the airplane will reach the field; if a field is not available, lower the flaps at any altitude.

CAUTION

Air speed must be high enough to prevent an inadvertent stall. (That is, if the flaps are to be retracted, it is advisable that the air speed be 10 knots higher than during normal approach while the flaps are down.)

e. DIVING FLAP CONTROL (Figure 7, Item 2).

(1) The diving flap selector lever (orange knob) controls the operation of the diving flaps. These flaps act as air brakes to retard the speed of the airplane during a dive.

CAUTION

Do not open the diving flaps if the landing flaps are partly open and the landing flap selector lever is in neutral. Opening the flaps will cause trapped fluid in the landing flap system to damage the flap-operating cylinder and linkage.

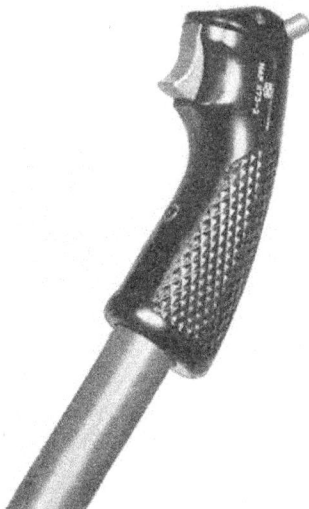

Figure 3—Pilot's Control Stick Handle

Figure 4—Tab Control Panel

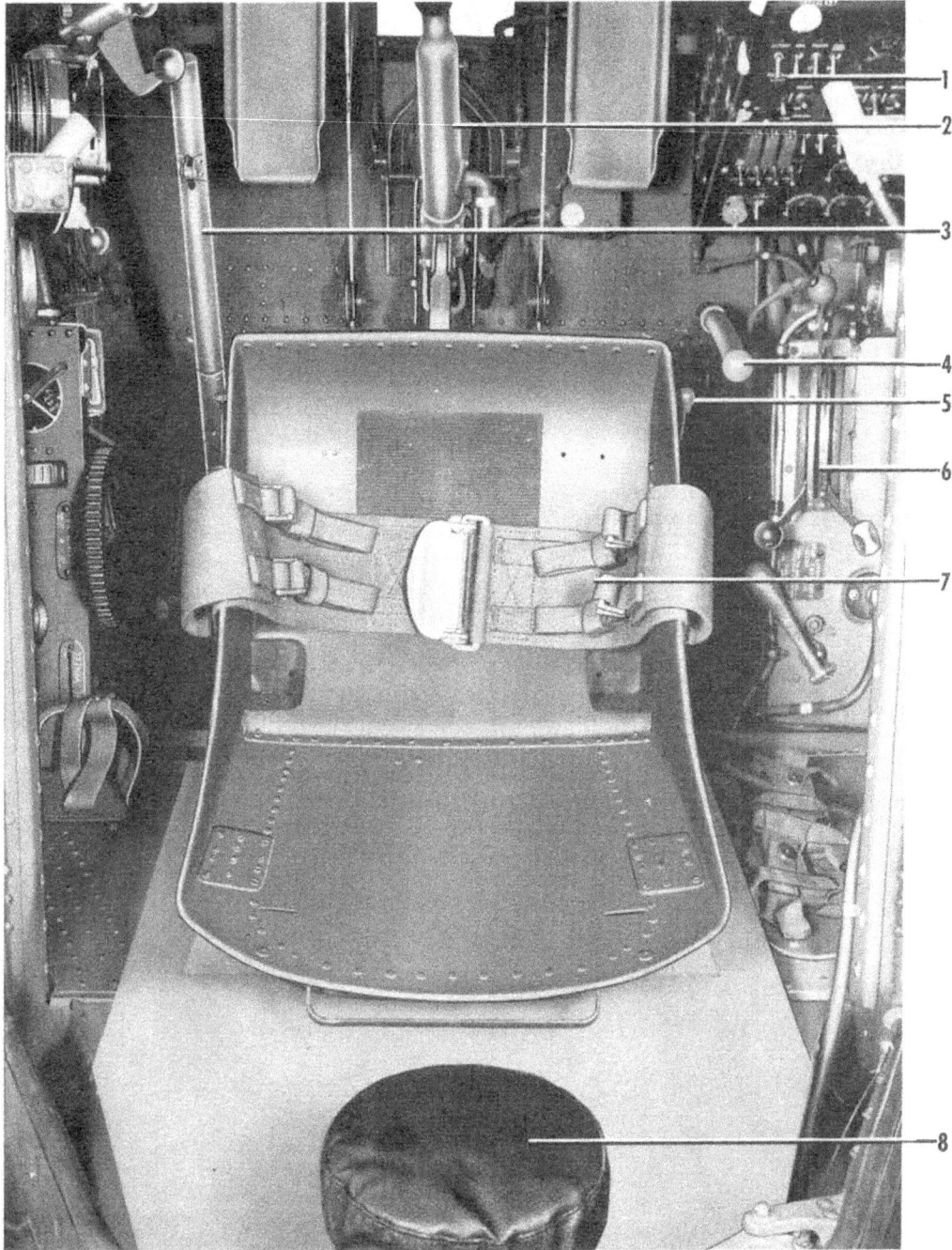

1 Electrical Distribution Panel
2 Control Stick
3 Arresting Hook Control
4 Hydraulic Hand Pump
5 Seat Adjustment Lever
6 Hydraulic Control Panel
7 Safety Belt
8 Headrest

Figure 5—Pilot's Cockpit—Top

1	Map Case	14	Throttle Control
2	Identification Radio Control Box	15	Throttle Radio Switch
3	Propeller Governor Control	16	Cowl Flap Control
4	Propeller Governor Adjustment Knob	17	Ignition Switch
5	Fuel Tank Selector Control	18	Mixture Control
6	Rudder Tab Control	19	Manual Bomb Release
7	Tail Wheel Lock	20	Bomb Release Button
8	Aileron Tab Control	21	Manual Arming Control
9	Elevator Tab Control	22	Landing Gear Position Indicator
10	Droppable Fuel Tank Selector Control	23	Control Stick Handle
11	Arresting Hook Control	24	Oil Cooler Scoop Control
12	Supercharger Control	25	Cockpit Ventilator Control
13	Parking Brake Control		

Figure 6—Pilot's Cockpit—Left Side

(2) **To open** the diving flaps, move the selector lever to the "OPEN" position and depress the engine pump control handle (Figure 7, Item 6). Normally, five seconds are required for this operation.

CAUTION

Do not open the diving flaps at an indicated air speed exceeding 210 knots.

(3) **To partially open** the diving flaps, move the selector lever to the "OPEN" position and depress the engine pump control handle (Figure 7, Item 6). When the flap indicator registers the desired position, return the selector lever to a neutral position (midway between "OPEN" and "CLOSED").

(4) **To close** the diving flaps, move the selector lever to the "CLOSED" position (the flaps close to a "trailing" position) and depress the engine pump control handle (Figure 7, Item 6) to completely close the flaps. Normally, one to two seconds are required for this operation.

NOTE

In case of engine pump failure, use the hydraulic hand pump (Figure 5, Item 4). Sixty strokes will result in 25 degrees of flap movement.

(5) Normally, the diving flap selector lever remains in the "CLOSED" position when the flaps are closed. However, in case of hydraulic line failure, place the selector lever in a neutral position to prevent the fluid in the reservoir from being pumped overboard.

CAUTION

When the airplane is parked, place the diving flap selector lever in the "CLOSED" position to allow any excessive hydraulic pressure, caused by temperature changes, to return to the reservoir.

f. SURFACE CONTROL LOCK. — The yoke-type surface control lock, on the floor forward of the pilot's control stick, locks the control surfaces in neutral. To engage the lock, remove the pin which holds the yoke to the floor, place both rudder pedals in neutral (directly opposite each other), unbutton the boot around the base of the control stick, lift the yoke and fasten it to the

fitting at the bottom of the control stick by means of the pin.

CAUTION

Secure the surface control lock to the floor during flight.

3. POWER PLANT CONTROLS.

The power plant controls are conventional for this airplane. They consist of the throttle control, propeller governor control, mixture control, supercharger control, carburetor air control, carburetor air filter control, cowl flap control, starter control, two fuel tank selector controls, ignition switch, primer switch, auxiliary fuel pump switch. Specific instructions for the use of these controls are given in Section II, "Power Plant."

The small button on top of the throttle control lever operates the pilot's throat microphone. An emergency throttle on the port side of the gunner's compartment operates in the same manner as the pilot's control and is the only auxiliary power plant control installed in the gunner's compartment.

4. AUXILIARY CONTROLS.

Auxiliary controls are those controls which are not absolutely necessary to maintain the airplane in flight. The majority of these controls, i.e., engine pump (hydraulic), landing gear, brakes, tail wheel, arresting hook, windshield heat, cockpit ventilator, and automatic pilot, are installed in the pilot's cockpit. However, other controls, such as the seat and pedal adjustment controls, enclosure latches, and the oxygen and radio equipment, are incorporated in the pilot's cockpit and the gunner's compartment.

a. HYDRAULIC RESERVOIR.—The hydraulic reservoir, located on the right side of the pilot's cockpit, aft of the fire wall, has an hydraulic fluid capacity of 148 cubic inches. A sight gage on the reservoir indicates the hydraulic fluid level. The reservoir supplies hydraulic fluid to the engine-driven pump, the hydraulic hand pump, and the master brake cylinders.

b. ENGINE PUMP (HYDRAULIC) CONTROL (Figure 7, Item 6).

(1) The engine-driven pump is mounted on the engine and directs fluid through a filter to the engine pump control valve (time delay valve).

(2) The engine pump control is aft of the landing and diving flap control quadrant and

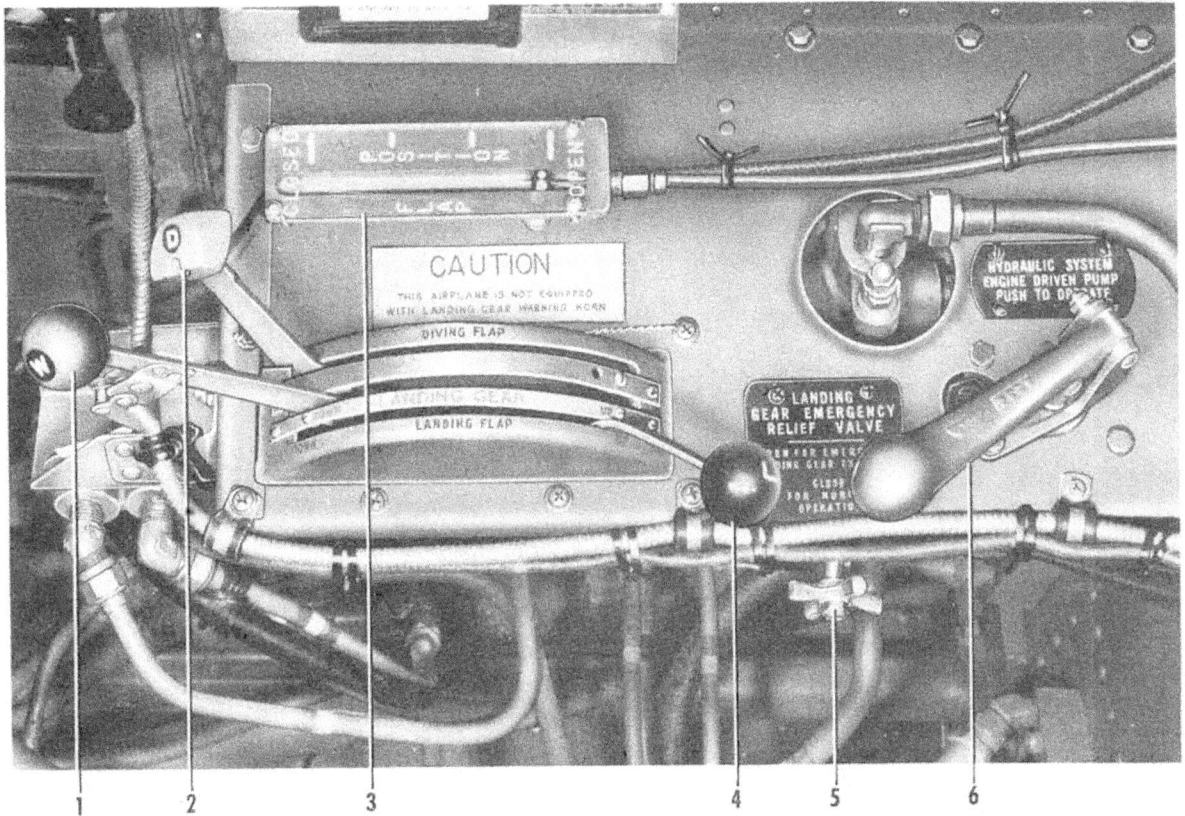

1 Landing Gear Control
2 Diving Flap Control
3 Flap Position Indicator
4 Landing Flap Control
5 Landing Gear Emergency Relief Valve
6 Engine Pump Control

Figure 7—Hydraulic Control Panel

Supply Line
Pressure Line
Return Line

VENT

FILLER CAP
STRAINER
FILTER

42 CU IN BELOW STANDPIPE
OPEN

ENGINE-DRIVEN
PUMP

CLOSED

FROM
SERVO UNITS

BYPASS
RELIEF VALVE

FILTER

RELIEF VALVE SET TO
HOLD 1050± 20 LB/SQ IN.

ENGINE PUMP
CONTROL VALVE

CHECK VALVE

RELIEF VALVE
SET TO HOLD
120 LB/SQ IN.

SPERRY RELIEF VALVE
(UNLOADER)

TO AUTO
PILOT

CHECK
VALVE

CLOSED

NEUTRAL

OPEN

COWLING FLAP
ACTUATING
CYLINDER

CHECK
VALVE

LANDING GEAR
EMERGENCY EXTEND
VALVE

EMERGENCY HAND PUMP

CHECK
VALVE

COWLING FLAP
SELECTOR VALVE

CLOSED

NEUTRAL

OPEN

RELIEF VALVE
SET TO HOLD
1350± 50 LB/SQ IN.

BRAKES OFF

HYDRAULIC BRAKE

MASTER BRAKE
CYLINDERS

HYDRAULIC BRAKE

DIVING FLAP CLOSED
WHEELS UP
LANDING FLAPS UP

GAGE GLASS

SELECTOR VALVE

W   D   L   W
          FORWARD   D

D   W   L

D

STRAINER
SEQUENCE
VALVE

BOOSTER CYLINDER

DIVING
FLAPS CLOSED

LANDING & DIVING FLAP
ACTUATING CYLINDER

LANDING
FLAPS UP

LANDING GEAR
LINK CONTROL
CYLS

GEAR UP
GEAR DOWN
GEAR UP

LANDING GEAR
ACTUATING CYLS

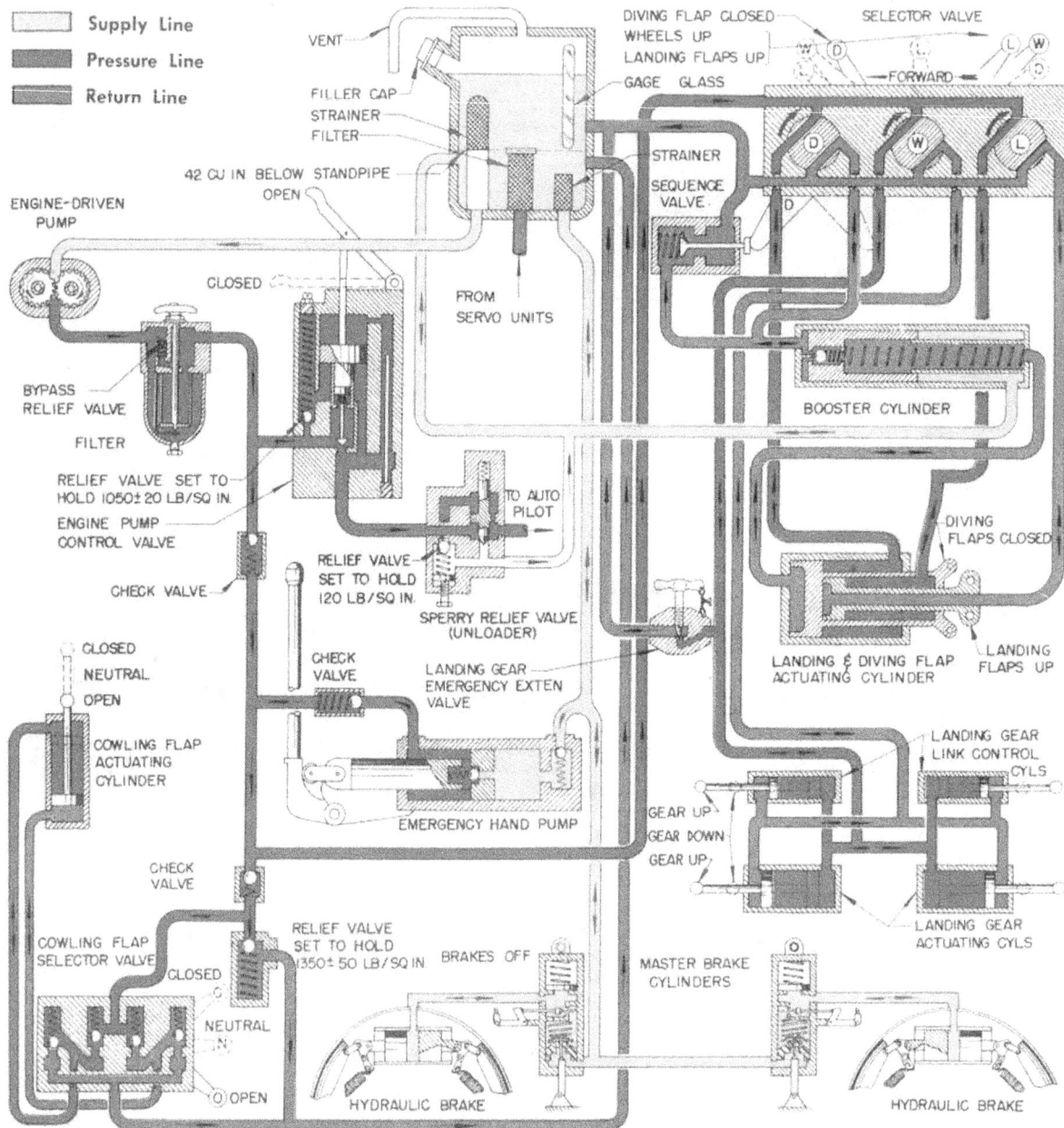

1. ENGINE PUMP CONTROL VALVE (TIME DELAY VALVE) OPEN — FREE FLOW
   TO THE RESERVOIR
2. ENGINE-DRIVEN HYDRAULIC PUMP OPERATING
3. LANDING GEAR UP
4. COWLING FLAPS OPEN
5. DIVING FLAPS CLOSED (SEQUENCE VALVE OPEN)
6. LANDING FLAPS UP

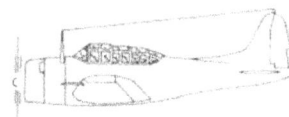

Figure 8—Hydraulic System

supplies the necessary pressure required to operate the hydraulically driven units. When the engine pump control handle is in the up, or normal, position, the fluid flows through a Sperry relief valve. This valve directs a fluid pressure of 120 psi to the automatic pilot; excess fluid returns to the reservoir.

NOTE

Depression of the engine pump control handle while the automatic pilot is on momentarily disrupts automatic pilot operation.

(3) When the engine pump control handle is depressed, the control valve maintains a pressure of approximately 1050 psi throughout the system to operate the landing flaps, diving flaps, cowl flaps, and landing gear. The engine pump control handle automatically returns to its normal position in 9 to 12 seconds.

NOTE

If the engine pump control handle does not automatically return to its normal position in approximately 15 seconds, return it manually.

c. HYDRAULIC HAND PUMP (Figure 5, Item 4).—The hydraulic hand pump is used in case of engine pump control failure. The hand pump, which supplies the necessary pressure to operate the actuating cylinders of the hydraulic units, is manually operated and is located to the right of the pilot's seat. To build up pressure in the hydraulic system, pump the hydraulic hand pump fore and aft until a sufficient pressure is attained to operate the desired unit.

d. HYDRAULIC CONTROL SYSTEM.

(1) Incorporated in the selector valves are the control levers for the landing flaps, diving flaps, landing gear, and cowl flaps. To operate any of these units, set the lever in the desired position and depress the engine pump control handle.

(2) Attached to the diving flap control lever is a sequence valve which permits immediate closing of the diving flaps to the trailing position. The booster cylinder, between the selector valve and the diving flap actuating cylinder, increases the normal hydraulic system pressure by a ratio of 2.7 to 1 to permit the diving flaps to be opened at an indicated air speed up to approximately 210 knots.

e. LANDING GEAR CONTROL (Figure 7, Item 1).

(1) The landing gear selector lever on the landing and diving flap control quadrant governs the operation of the landing gear for take-off and landing.

CAUTION

If the selector lever freezes, **force** it to the "DOWN" position and open the landing gear emergency relief valve. This operation releases hydraulic fluid from the actuating cylinders into the return lines. From the return lines the fluid flows back to the reservoir and the landing gear extends by its own weight.

(2) The landing gear selector lever should remain in the full "UP" or full "DOWN" position at all times so that the safety latch, connected to the selector lever, locks the gear in either the completely extended or completely retracted position. Immediately to the left of the left rudder pedal is an indicator which registers the position of the landing gear.

(3) **To retract** the landing gear, move the selector lever to the "UP" position and depress the engine pump control handle. Normally, six seconds are required for this operation.

NOTE

In case of engine pump failure, use the hydraulic hand pump (Figure 5, Item 4).

(4) **To extend** the landing gear, move the selector lever to the "DOWN" position. The landing gear should lower and lock within six seconds as registered on the indicator. The landing gear shall not be used to reduce speed during dives and, except in an emergency, shall not be extended at speeds exceeding 125 knots. (Refer to the note following Paragraph 1. in Section IV.)

EMERGENCY

If one or both landing gears will not extend when the landing gear selector lever is moved to the "DOWN" position, apply pressure to the system by operating the engine pump control handle.

If this operation does not actuate the landing gear, relieve pressure by shifting the cowl flap control to either the "OPEN" or the "CLOSED" position and then back to "NEUTRAL." Reapply pressure to the system by operating the emergency hand pump.

If the strut is still not free, move the landing gear selector lever to the "UP" position, apply pressure to the system to bring the landing gear to the fully retracted position, and repeat the above emergency procedure to extend the landing gear.

If this procedure fails, bleed the landing gear hydraulic actuating system by breaking the safety wire and opening the emergency relief valve (Figure 7, Item 5). Place the landing gear selector lever in the "DOWN" position and execute maneuvers that develop negative acceleration of approximately two load factors. If the strut does not extend, execute negative accelerations of approximately two load factors, followed immediately by a snap pull-out of approximately five load factors.

Before other hydraulic units can function normally, the emergency relief valve must be closed.

f. LANDING GEAR EMERGENCY RELIEF VALVE (Figure 7, Item 5).

(1) The landing gear emergency relief valve is below the engine pump control handle. This valve releases hydraulic pressure from the landing gear actuating cylinder to enable the landing gear to extend by gravity and bungee action. Use this valve only when the landing gear does not extend in the normal manner.

(2) To open the landing gear emergency relief valve, turn the control handle counterclockwise to permit the fluid to return to the reservoir. When the landing gear has been extended and locked, turn the control handle clockwise.

NOTE

The landing gear emergency relief valve is safetied by means of a wire which must be broken by hand before the valve can be used.

g. TAIL WHEEL (SWIVEL) LOCK (Figure 6, Item 7).

(1) The tail wheel lock is unlocked for all carrier operations, except when the airplane is

parked, and is locked for airfield landings and take-offs.

(2) To unlock the tail wheel, move the lever forward to the "RELEASED" position; to lock the tail wheel, move the lever aft to the "LOCKED" position.

h. ARRESTING HOOK CONTROL (Figure 6, Item 11).

(1) The arresting hook control lever is left of the pilot's seat and is used for carrier deck landings only. Lock the control lever in the full "HOOK UP" or full "HOOK DOWN" position at all times.

(2) To lower the arresting hook, move the control lever aft to the "HOOK DOWN" position; to stow the arresting hook, move the control lever forward to the "HOOK UP" position.

CAUTION

Lock the control lever in the "HOOK "DOWN" position prior to carrier landings.

i. APPROACH LIGHT.

(1) The Type 1-A approach light in the leading edge of the left wing operates in conjunction with the arresting hook. When the arresting hook is extended, the approach light automatically illuminates and indicates to the signal officer the attitude of the airplane in respect to carrier landing as follows: red light, too low; green light, too high; amber light, correct approach. The illumination of the approach light also indicates to the signal officer that the arresting hook is lowered.

(2) When a landing is made on an airfield (arresting hook retracted), the approach light can be operated by the switch (Figure 14, Item 8) on the pilot's electrical distribution panel.

j. BRAKES (Figure 2, Item 8).—The hydraulic wheel brakes are operated by depressing the upper portion of the rudder pedals. To operate the brakes, depress either or both brake treadles.

CAUTION

Do not pump the brakes except in an emergency.

k. PARKING BRAKE CONTROL (Figure 9).—The parking brake control is left of the pilot's instrument panel. This control is used to apply constant braking while the airplane is at rest on the

Figure 9—Parking Brake Control

ground. The control operates in conjunction with the brake treadles as follows:

(1) To apply the parking brakes, depress the brake treadles, pull out the parking brake control handle, and rotate it one-quarter turn; then release the brake treadles.

(2) To release the parking brakes, turn the control handle one-quarter turn, push it in, and depress the brake treadles.

CAUTION

Do not pump the brakes except in an emergency.

l. RUDDER PEDAL ADJUSTMENT (Figure 2, Item 20).—Adjustment treadles, incorporated on the inboard edge of each rudder pedal, permit the pedals to be adjusted to the stature and comfort of the pilot or gunner. To adjust the rudder pedals, apply downward toe pressure on the treadles to release the locks; then move the pedals fore and aft until they occupy the desired position.

m. BRAKE PEDAL ADJUSTMENT (Figure 2, Item 17).—Adjustment levers, incorporated on the inboard edge of each brake pedal, permit the pedals to be adjusted to the stature and comfort of the pilot. To adjust the brake pedals, apply side foot pressure on the levers to release the locks; then move the pedals fore and aft until they occupy the desired position.

n. PILOT'S SEAT ADJUSTMENT (Figure 5, Item 5).—The pilot's seat adjustment lever, attached to the upper right side of the seat, permits the seat to be adjusted to the proper height. Lift and hold the adjusting lever while raising or lowering the seat by body weight; release the lever to lock the seat in place.

o. GUNNER'S SEAT ADJUSTMENTS. — The gunner's seat can be adjusted for height, swivel, and tilt as follows:

(1) The height adjustment lever (Figure 29, Item 4) is forward of the left armor plate, adjacent to the swivel track, and permits the seat to be raised or lowered by body weight. Release the lever to lock the seat in position.

(2) The locking pin (Figure 29, Item 2) is below the height adjustment lever and permits the seat to swivel or lock in a fore and aft position. To release the lock, depress the lever and rotate it one-quarter turn.

(3) Adjust the seat for tilt when the gunner faces aft only. Downward pressure on the foot pedal (Figure 32, Item 3) behind the right foot brace permits the seat to be tilted.

p. GUNNER'S ARMOR PLATE ADJUSTMENT.—Locking pins (Figure 29, Items 1 and 5) for the gunner's chest armor plate are installed

Figure 10—Fixed Gun Sight

on each side of the seat fittings. To lock the plates, bring them together, allow the pins to lock in place, and fasten the plates with the latch cord. To open the plates, lift and turn the locking pins one-quarter turn, and push the plates down as they are opened.

NOTE

The plates cannot be opened if the seat is at its lowest adjustment.

q. **WINDSHIELD HEAT CONTROL (Figure 2, Item 2).**—The windshield heat control handle is above the upper instrument panel. This control allows hot air to circulate over the windshield to clear it of ice and fog. Pull out the control handle to open the windshield heat control; push the handle in to close the heat control.

r. **COCKPIT VENTILATOR CONTROL (Figure 2, Item 18).**—The cockpit ventilator control is beneath the lower instrument panel, to the right of the control stick. Outside air is admitted by means of a butterfly valve incorporated in the ventilator tube. Operate the control by thumb pressure.

s. **ENCLOSURE LATCHES.** — The enclosure latches can be operated from either inside or outside the enclosure.

(1) The inside latch for the **pilot's enclosure** is on the upper right edge of the enclosure; the outside latch is on the bottom right corner of the enclosure. Raise the outside lever or pull down on the inside lever to permit the enclosure to slide and lock in any of its five positions.

(2) The **gunner's enclosure** is divided into two sections: forward and aft. The forward enclosure has two positions: it is operated from the inside by a latch on the right side, just below the enclosure track, and from the outside by a latch below the fore part of the section. The aft section of the enclosure is released by a handle near the upper right inside corner. To slide the aft section forward, depress the handle, tilt the section, and slide it under the center enclosure. The latch, which is used to operate the forward section, also releases the aft section for replacement.

t. **OXYGEN SYSTEM.**—This model airplane is equipped with either a diluter-demand oxygen system or an oxygen rebreathing system. Those airplanes which are equipped with the rebreathing system will be service-changed to a diluter-demand system.

(1) **DILUTER-DEMAND OXYGEN SYSTEM.**—A separate diluter-demand system is provided for the pilot and for the gunner. All personnel using oxygen equipment should familiarize themselves thoroughly with the symptoms of anoxia as described in Technical Note No. 30-41 so that they may be on the alert at all times to detect oxygen deficiencies before serious physical effects have resulted.

(a) **OXYGEN CYLINDER.** — The oxygen cylinder which supplies both systems is located on the right side of the gunner's compartment. The cylinder has a capacity of 514 cubic inches. The main shut-off valve is on top of the cylinder.

(b) **OXYGEN REGULATORS (Figure 11).**

1. The oxygen regulator for the pilot is to the right of the seat. The oxygen regulator for the gunner is forward of the oxygen cylinder on the right side of the gunner's compartment. The diluter-demand regulator operates in conjunction with normal respiration to supply correct amounts of oxygen at all altitudes. At low levels, only a small amount of oxygen is delivered because the atmosphere contains sufficient oxygen; at approximately 30,000 feet, 100 percent oxygen is required and is delivered on demand.

2. The oxygen pressure gage (Figure 11, Item 4), located on the aft section of the regulator, registers the correct amount of oxygen pressure.

3. The oxygen diluter control (Figure 11, Item 2) is on the lower section of the regulator. When the control is in the "ON" position, the regulator will automatically select the correct oxygen-air mixture. When the control is in the "OFF" position, pure oxygen is supplied on demand. The control should be "ON" for normal operations.

4. The oxygen emergency control (red knob) (Figure 11, Item 3) is below the pressure gage. When the knob is turned counterclockwise, pure oxygen is delivered in a steady flow. When the knob is turned clockwise, the flow will cease. The emergency control should be used in an emergency or when the diluter-demand regulator becomes inoperative. When using the emergency control, open it slowly to obtain the minimum flow required.

(c) **OXYGEN MASKS.** — The Type 14 demand oxygen mask is provided with straps for attachment to the helmet. The mask should be fitted to the helmet, adjusted to the wearer, and tested for leakage.

1 To Oxygen Mask
2 Oxygen Diluter Control
3 Oxygen Emergency Control
4 Cylinder Pressure Gage
5 To Oxygen Cylinder

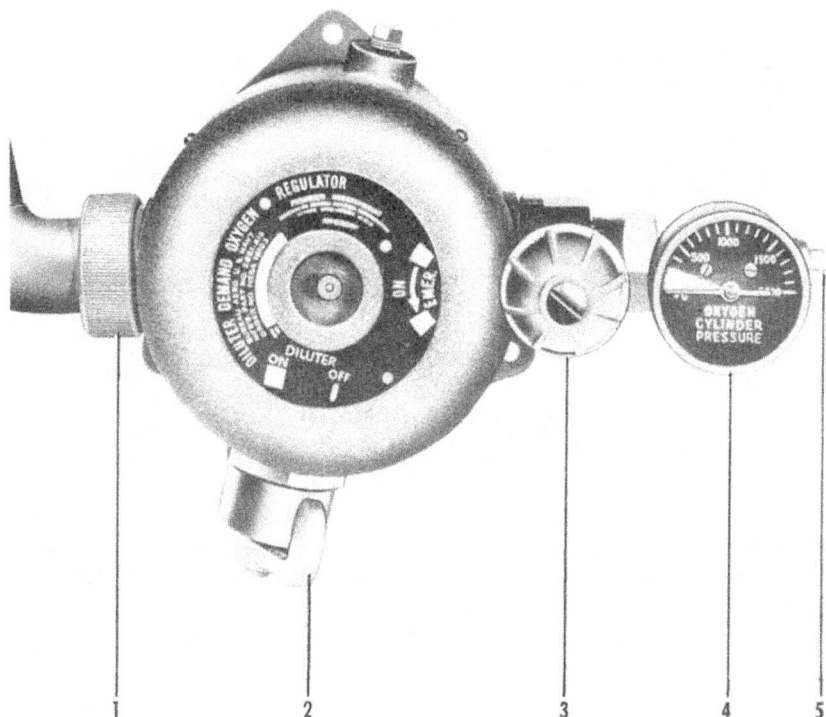

Figure 11—Diluter-Demand Oxygen Regulator

(d) PREFLIGHT CHECK OF DILUTER-DEMAND OXYGEN SYSTEM. — In order to assure proper functioning of the oxygen system during a flight in which oxygen is to be used or is likely to be used, the following items shall be checked prior to flight while the airplane is on the ground.

1. Check the emergency valve to make certain that it is **closed**.

2. Open the cylinder valve and allow at least 10 seconds for the pressure in the line to equalize. The pressure gage should indicate 1800 ±50 psi if the cylinder is fully charged.

3. Close the cylinder valve. After a few minutes, observe the pressure gage and simultaneously open the cylinder valve. If the gage pointer jumps, leakage is indicated.

NOTE

If leakage was indicated in the preceding step, open the cylinder valve and carefully note the pressure gage reading; then close the cylinder valve. **If the gage pointer drops more than 100 psi in five**

minutes, there is excessive leakage and the system must be repaired prior to use.

4. Check the mask fit by placing a thumb over the end of the mask tube and inhaling lightly. If there is no leakage, the mask will adhere to the face as a result of the suction created. If the mask leaks, tighten the suspension straps and adjust the nose wire. **Do not use a mask that leaks.**

5. Couple the mask securely to the breathing tube by means of the quick-disconnect coupling. **THE MATING PARTS OF THE COUPLING MUST NOT BE COCKED, BUT MUST BE FULLY ENGAGED.**

6. Open the cylinder valve and depress the diaphragm knob through the hole in the center of the regulator case. Release the diaphragm knob. Breathe several times and observe the oxygen-flow indicator (if installed) for blinking, which verifies a positive flow of oxygen.

NOTE

Since the amount of added oxygen is very small at sea level, the oxygen-flow indicator may not operate while the airplane is on the ground. In this case, turn the air-valve to "OFF" (100 percent oxygen) and test again. If the oxygen-flow indicator now operates satisfactorily, reset the air-valve to the "ON" (normal oxygen) position. This setting will now supply an adequate oxygen flow and correct blinker operation when needed.

7. Test the emergency valve by turning it counterclockwise slowly until the oxygen flows vigorously into the mask; then close the emergency valve.

8. Upon completion of the flight, turn the cylinder valve off.

(e) OPERATION OF DILUTER-DEMAND OXYGEN EQUIPMENT.

1. Open the oxygen cylinder valve. The pressure gage should indicate 1800 ± 50 psi if the cylinder is fully charged.

2. Set the air-valve to the "ON" (normal oxygen) position, except when the presence of excessive carbon monoxide is suspected, in which case, set the air-valve to the "OFF" (100 percent oxygen) position.

3. Put on the oxygen mask; make certain that the quick-disconnect coupling is **fully** engaged.

4. Check the mask fit by squeezing the mask tube and inhaling lightly. Suction will cause the mask to adhere tightly to the face if there is no leakage. If the mask leaks, tighten the mask suspension straps.

CAUTION

Do not check the mask fit by squeezing the mask tube while the emergency valve is "ON."

5. Breathe normally and observe the oxygen flow indicator (if installed); blinking verifies positive flow of oxygen.

6. Check the cylinder pressure gage frequently for available oxygen supply and the oxygen flow indicator (if installed) for flow of oxygen to the mask.

7. Use oxygen on the following flights:

a. On all flights above 10,000 feet.

CAUTION

If the system should fail, quickly descend

to at least 15,000 feet. Unconsciousness occurs in a very short time at higher altitudes.

b. For a minimum of fifteen minutes out of every hour on all flights of more than four hours at an altitude of 8,000 to 10,000 feet.

c. On night flights above 5,000 feet; personnel whose acuity of night vision is not essential may be excepted.

NOTE

In aircraft provided with diluter-demand regulators, the air-valve shall be set to the "ON" (normal oxygen) position. However, if the presence of excessive carbon monoxide is suspected, the air-valve shall be set to the "OFF" (100 percent oxygen) position until the flight has been completed.

(2) OXYGEN REBREATHING SYSTEM.—An oxygen rebreathing system of the central supply type is installed in the pilot's cockpit and in the gunner's compartment. This system, which is used for breathing in high altitudes, consists of the oxygen bottle, the rebreathing units, and the canisters.

(a) OXYGEN BOTTLE. — The oxygen supply bottle for both rebreathers is on the aft right side of the gunner's compartment. A valve on the top of the bottle controls the supply of oxygen.

(b) REBREATHERS AND FACEPIECE. —The rebreathing unit incorporates a facepiece through which the wearer breathes. The pilot's rebreather is stowed above the engine pump control; the gunner's rebreather is above the oxygen bottle. Tubes leading from the oxygen bottle supply the necessary oxygen to both rebreathers.

(c) CANISTERS. — A holder on the left side of the rebreather case clamps the canisters in place and permits them to be easily replaced. The canisters, which purify exhaled air, are inserted only when they are to be used and **after** the tear-off caps have been removed. The pilot's two canisters are stowed in brackets on the right side of the seat; one of the gunner's canisters is left of the rebreather; the other is stowed above the tail pipe valve. Make certain that the facepiece shut-off valve is closed before inserting a fresh canister. Be careful that no foreign matter finds its way into the mechanism.

NOTE

Replace the canisters every two hours if

the tear-off caps have been removed. If the metal cap seal is broken, do not use the canister.

(d) OXYGEN EQUIPMENT PREFLIGHT CHECK.

1. Attach the rebreather apparatus to the central system supply line.

2. Check the hose connections at the apparatus for tightness. These connections should be tightened with the special wrench provided. Finger tight is not sufficient to obtain adequate sealing.

3. Depress the facepiece valve and put the knob clamp in place.

4. Open the oxygen cylinder valve and allow the breathing bag to fill. The high-pressure gage on the pressure reducer should read 1800 ± 50 psi if the cylinder is fully charged. Close the oxygen cylinder valve and watch the high-pressure gage. If the high-pressure gage needle falls, a high-pressure leak is indicated at the coupling connector between the reducer and cylinder or in the reducer. If a high-pressure cylinder leak is not found, open the oxygen cylinder valve again. Depress the admission valve by finger pressure through the rebreather case and admit additional oxygen to fill the breathing bag to the edge of the case. The bag should inflate in 5 to 10 seconds. Close the cylinder valve and press the admission valve lever arm. If the bag deflates under this pressure, a leak is indicated in the hose connections, the facepiece shut-off valve, or the canister holder sealing valves.

5. Install a canister after removing the sealing caps from each end. Open the oxygen supply valve.

6. Retest for tightness to check the canister seal.

7. Put on the facepiece. Release the knob clamp and place the facepiece valve in the normal operating position.

8. Check the fit of the mask by squeezing the corrugated breathing tube and inhaling lightly. The mask will collapse if there is no leakage. DO NOT USE A MASK THAT LEAKS.

9. Flush out the apparatus as follows:

a. Inhale deeply from the breathing bag. (The facepiece valve knob is released and sprung outward.)

CAUTION

Do NOT inhale when the facepiece valve is depressed.

b. Depress the facepiece valve knob and exhale completely to the outside atmosphere.

c. Repeat this procedure until a total of three successive inhalations have been exhaled to the outside atmosphere.

d. Allow the facepiece valve knob to remain in the outward position and begin to breathe normally into and out of the apparatus.

e. Repeat the above flushing procedure after 5, 15, and 30 minutes' operation and every 30 minutes thereafter.

NOTE

During the above flushing procedure, extreme care must be taken to prevent any outside air from entering the breathing system.

10. Replace the canister when it offers excessive resistance to exhalation. However, increased resistance to exhalation may be caused by an over-filled breathing bag; therefore, it is best to employ procedures a. and b. of Paragraph 9., above. If excessive resistance to exhalation continues after venting one breath, the canister should be changed. Normal canister life is approximately two hours.

11. Immediately after replacing the canister, perform steps a., b., and c. of Paragraph 9., above; repeat these steps every half hour thereafter.

12. Before stowing the rebreathing apparatus, release the facepiece valve clamp.

13. Close the oxygen cylinder valve.

NOTE

All personnel using oxygen equipment should familiarize themselves thoroughly with the symptoms of anoxia as described in Technical Note No. 30-41 so that they may be on the alert, at all times, to detect oxygen deficiencies before serious physical effects occur.

u. AUTOMATIC PILOT SYSTEM. — The control for the automatic pilot is installed above the electrical distribution panel (Figure 2, Item 13). The automatic pilot instruments (Figure 12) are

1 Rudder Signal Adjustment
2 Course-setting Knob
3 Aileron Signal Adjustment
4 Bank-and-Climb Gyro
5 Elevator Signal Adjustment
6 Caging Knob
7 Caging Knob
8 Directional Gyro
9 Aileron Trim Knob
10 Miniature Airplane Adjustment Knob
11 Elevator Trim Knob

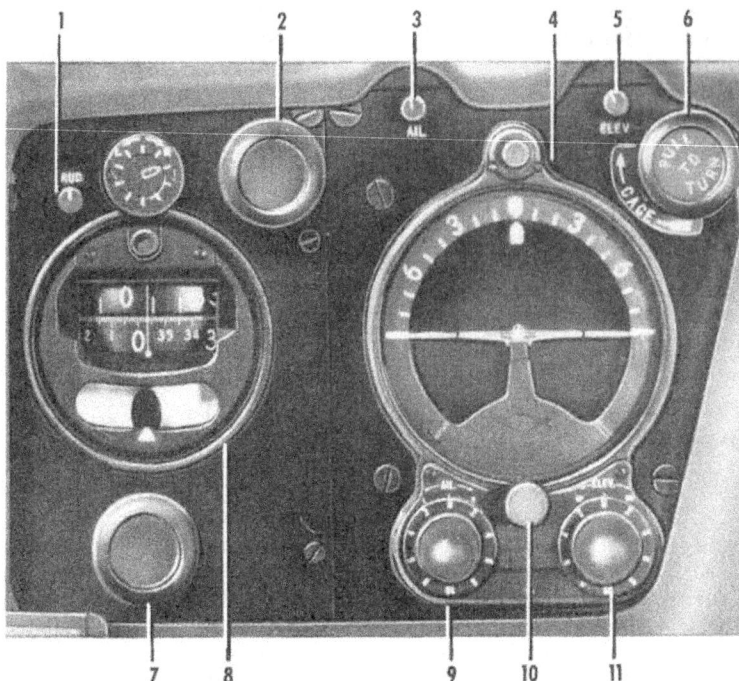

Figure 12—Automatic Pilot Control Instruments

on the instrument panel. The automatic pilot system is used to fly the airplane at a fixed attitude of flight by means of the directional gyro and the bank-and-climb gyro.

(1) **OPERATION OF THE TRANSFER VALVE AND THE SERVO UNITS.**—Incorporated in the system are the Sperry transfer valve and the servo unit which operates as follows:

(a) The Sperry transfer valve transforms air impulses from the gyroscopic instruments to oil impulses which actuate the servo units.

(b) The servo units receive the oil impulses and actuate the aileron, rudder, and elevator control cables.

(2) **OPERATION OF THE AUTOMATIC PILOT.** — The automatic pilot is operated as follows:

(a) Check the automatic pilot oil pressure gage (Figure 33, Item 15); it should indicate approximately 120 psi pressure at 1000 rpm.

(b) Proceed as follows before engaging the automatic pilot:

1. Set the lower, or directional, card on the directional gyro control unit at the magnetic

compass reading by pushing in and turning the caging knob.

2. Uncage the directional gyro by pulling the caging knob straight out.

3. Turn the course-setting knob until the upper, or reference, card coincides with the directional gyro.

4. Uncage the bank-and-climb gyro control unit by pulling out the caging knob and turning it counterclockwise as far as possible. (Push the knob in to lock the control in this position.)

5. Turn the aileron and elevator trim knobs on the bank-and-climb control unit until the pointers on the index dials register zero.

6. Trim the airplane for "hands off" condition.

7. **Engage** the automatic pilot by turning the control "ON."

CAUTION

The automatic pilot control must not be left in an intermediate position at any time.

(c) After the automatic pilot is in operation, adjust the course-setting knob and the aileron and elevator trim knobs slightly, if necessary, to place the airplane in straight, level flight. Rapidity of control response is regulated by the knurled signal adjustment knobs.

(d) Before entering combat or acrobatics, place the automatic pilot control in the "OFF" position, and cage the directional and the bank-and-climb control units.

(3) **MANEUVERS.**

(a) **TO MAKE A TURN.**

1. Set the desired fore and aft attitude by means of the elevator trim knob.

2. Change the course by **slowly** turning the course-setting knob. If a sharp turn is being made, bank the airplane by turning the aileron trim knob.

(b) **TO MAKE A CAGED TURN.**

1. Cage the directional gyro control unit by pushing the caging knob straight in.

2. Turn the course-setting knob (a maximum of 10 degrees is permitted) in the desired direction.

3. Set the airplane in a bank, by means of the aileron trim knob, in order to bring the inclinometer ball to a central position.

(c) **TO STOP A CAGED TURN.**

1. Remove the bank by turning the aileron trim knob until the inclinometer ball is again in a central position.

2. Align the upper card with the lower card by turning the course-setting knob.

3. Uncage the directional gyro by pulling the caging knob straight out.

(4) **OPERATING LIMITS OF THE AUTOMATIC PILOT.**

(a) **CLIMBING OR GLIDING.**—When operating the airplane **automatically**, do not exceed 27 degrees in either direction if the bank-and-climb instrument bears Part No. 648045 or Part No. 643580M. If the instrument bears neither of these **complete** part numbers, do not exceed 18 degrees in either direction. When operating the airplane **manually** while the gyros are acting as flight instruments only, do not exceed 55 degrees in either direction.

CAUTION

If the flight reference limits (55 degrees) are to be still exceeded, cage the gyros while the airplane is still in level flight.

(b) **BANKING.**—When operating the airplane **automatically**, do not exceed 25 degrees in either direction. When operating the airplane **manually** while the gyros are acting as flight instruments only, **do not exceed** the following limits:

Directional Gyro ....55 degrees
Bank-and-Climb Gyro ......90 degrees

CAUTION

If the flight reference limits are to be exceeded, cage the gyros while the airplane is still in level flight.

(c) **TURNING.** — The amount of turn which can be made is unlimited.

(5) **AUTOMATIC PILOT GROUND CHECK.**

(a) **OIL IN THE RESERVOIR.**—Quantity should be normal. To check the operation of the vacuum and oil pumps, set the engine at 600 to 700 rpm; tee-in a vacuum gage at the gyro instruments. The gage should read four to five inches Hg.

(b) **OIL PRESSURE.** — The oil pressure should be 115 to 125 psi while the automatic pilot is "ON" and the engine is running at 1000 rpm.

(c) **TESTING FOR AIR IN THE SYSTEM.** —Place the automatic pilot in the "ON" position; set the gyro trim knobs at zero; note sponginess in the controls; controls should **react** as though locked under light control force. Place the elevators in the down position by means of the elevator control knob on the gyro unit. Apply light pressure to the control stick in the opposite direction. Sponginess in the control indicates air in the system. Use the rudder and aileron control knobs and repeat the above procedure.

(d) **BLEEDING AIR FROM THE SYSTEM.**—Run the engine at 1000 rpm; set the automatic pilot to "OFF." Apply a signal to each transfer valve diaphragm by rotating each gyro trim knob at least one-half turn. Leave the trim knob in this position. Eliminate air by holding each control in the extreme position for 30 seconds to allow air to travel from the servo to the reservoir. Do not mistake springing of the control cables for the resilient action of air in a servo

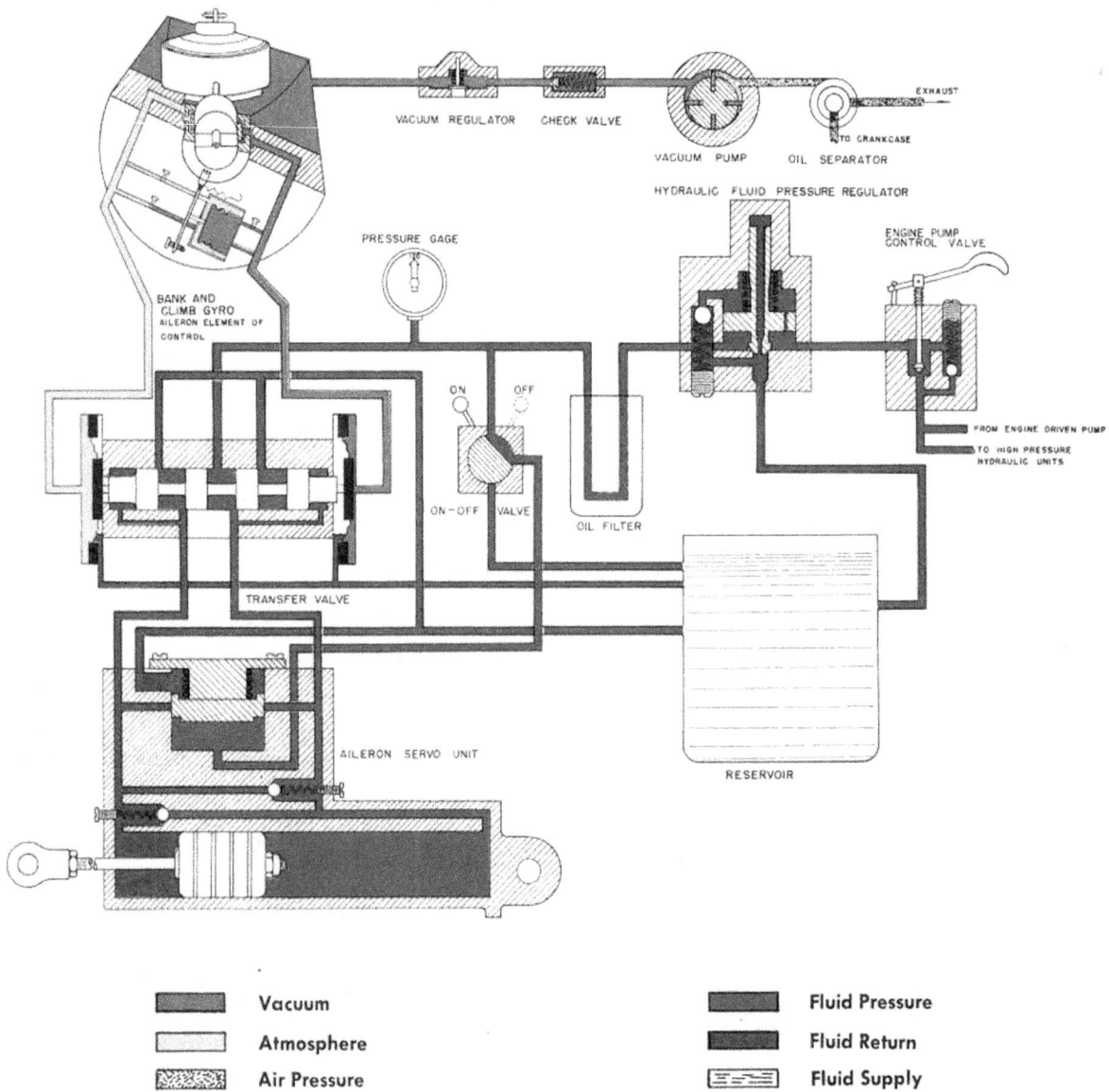

VACUUM REGULATOR   CHECK VALVE

VACUUM PUMP   OIL SEPARATOR

EXHAUST

TO CRANKCASE

HYDRAULIC FLUID PRESSURE REGULATOR

ENGINE PUMP
CONTROL VALVE

PRESSURE GAGE

BANK AND
CLIMB GYRO
AILERON ELEMENT OF
CONTROL

ON   OFF

ON-OFF VALVE   OIL FILTER

FROM ENGINE DRIVEN PUMP

TO HIGH PRESSURE
HYDRAULIC UNITS

TRANSFER VALVE

RESERVOIR

AILERON SERVO UNIT

	Vacuum		Fluid Pressure
	Atmosphere		Fluid Return
	Air Pressure		Fluid Supply

NOTE: AUTOMATIC PILOT ENGAGED,
BANK-AND-CLIMB GYRO CONTROL
SHOWN CORRECTING A BANK

Figure 13—Automatic Pilot System

cylinder. Center the controls; uncage the gyros; set the gyro trim knobs at neutral; turn the automatic pilot control valve "ON." The controls should remain in position.

(e) AIRPLANE CONTROLS. — Note the neutral position of the airplane controls; run the engine at 1000 rpm; center the airplane controls; uncage the gyros; set the gyro trim knobs at zero; turn the automatic pilot "ON." Readjust the trim knobs until the controls are in the neutral position. The controls should remain in this position.

(f) CONTROL SURFACES.

1. Note the direction and speed of movement; move the gyro trim knobs back and forth; each control should move in the proper direction and at approximately equal speed each way.

2. Turn the **aileron trim knob** clockwise —right aileron up (control stick moves to the right).

3. Turn the **elevator trim knob** clockwise —elevator down (control stick moves forward).

4. Turn the **course-setting knob** clockwise—right rudder (right rudder pedal moves forward).

(g) SERVO OVERPOWER RELIEF VALVES.

1. Apply light pressure to the controls; simultaneously apply automatic pilot force in the opposite direction by means of the gyro trim knobs; the controls should move against the light pressure.

2. Note the force necessary to overpower the automatic pilot; set the servo unit relief valve for 105 psi pressure; the automatic pilot should be overpowered with the following approximate forces on the airplane controls:

Aileron ....28.5 lb on stick
Elevator ....28.5 lb on stick
Rudder ....103.0 lb on rudder pedal

(6) AUTOMATIC PILOT FLIGHT CHECK.

(a) Use the gyros as regular flight instruments and fly the airplane to an altitude of 2000 feet.

(b) Check the oil pressure; it should be 115 to 125 psi.

(c) Trim the airplane for straight, level flight and align both gyro instruments.

(d) Slowly turn the automatic pilot control valve "ON."

(e) Overpower each control in each direction to assure overpowering of the automatic pilot.

(f) Adjust the automatic pilot signal to maximum (clockwise) and slowly decrease the signal as required for best performance and to eliminate over-controlling.

(g) Fly the airplane to an altitude where varying air currents and rough air are present; check the signal adjustments.

(h) Climb to the maximum ceiling at which the automatic pilot is used; check the operation and required oil pressure.

(i) Retard the throttle to approximately 1000 rpm and check the automatic pilot in a glide; note the minimum rpm required for satisfactory operation.

(j) Fly a straight course; use a magnetic compass to check the directional gyro at intervals; a deviation of four degrees in 15 minutes is permissible.

(k) Rotate the rudder knob and make a slow 180-degree turn; check the precision of the gyros. Also check a slow 360-degree turn.

(l) Check the artificial horizon for return to normal.

(m) During severe maneuvers, cage the automatic pilot gyros.

v. ELECTRICAL DISTRIBUTION PANELS.

(1) The **pilot's** electrical distribution panel (Figure 14) is on the lower right side of the cockpit and contains the following: volt-ammeter with selector switch; battery and generator switches; fuel pump and engine primer switches; switches for the exterior, recognition, approach, instrument, and cockpit lights; thermometer and pitot heater control switches; rheostats for the gun sight, instrument lights, distribution panel lights, and chartboard lights; gun, gun sight, bomb, camera, and arming switches; exterior lights master switch and radio master switch; and a receptacle and switch. A spare lamp box is installed above the electrical distribution panel, to the left of the automatic pilot control.

(2) The **gunner's** electrical distribution panel (Figure 15) is located on the right side of the compartment and contains the following: switches

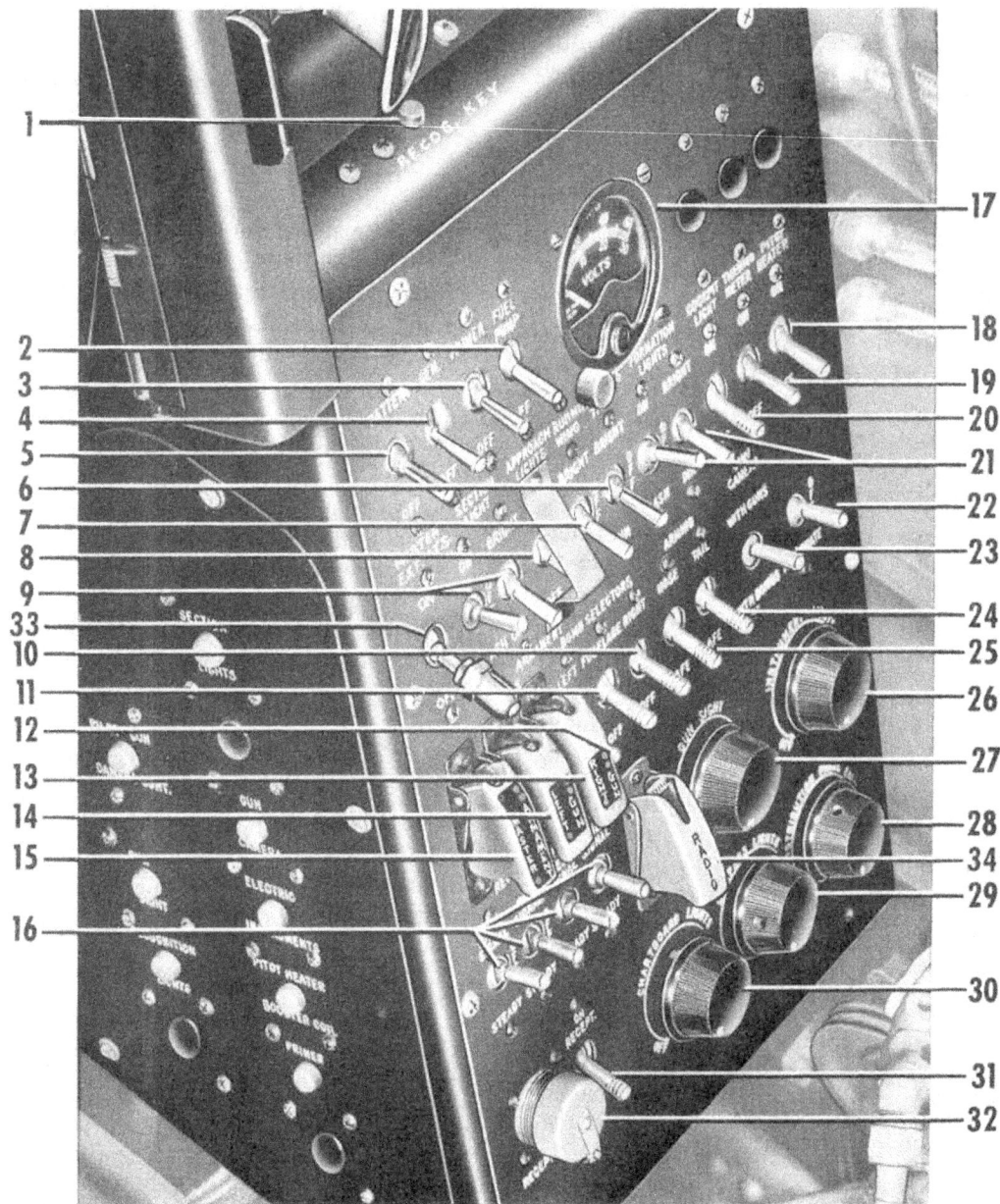

Figure 14—Pilot's Electrical Distribution Panel

1 Recognition Light Key	10 Right Bomb Selector	18 Pitot Heater	26 Instrument Light Rheostat
2 Auxiliary Fuel Pump	11 Fuselage Bomb Selector	19 Thermometer	27 Gun Sight Rheostat
3 Primer	12 Left Bomb Selector	20 Cockpit Lights	28 Distribution Panel Light Rheostat
4 Generator	13 Right Gun Selector	21 Formation Lights	29 Compass Light Rheostat
5 Battery	14 Left Gun Selector	22 Gun Sight	30 Chartboard Lights Rheostat
6 Tail Running Light	15 Master Armament	23 Gun Camera	31 Receptacle Switch
7 Wing Running Lights	16 Recognition Lights	24 Tail Arming	32 Receptacle
8 Approach Light	17 Volt-ammeter	25 Nose Arming	33 Exterior Lights Master Switch
9 Section Light			34 Radio Master Switch

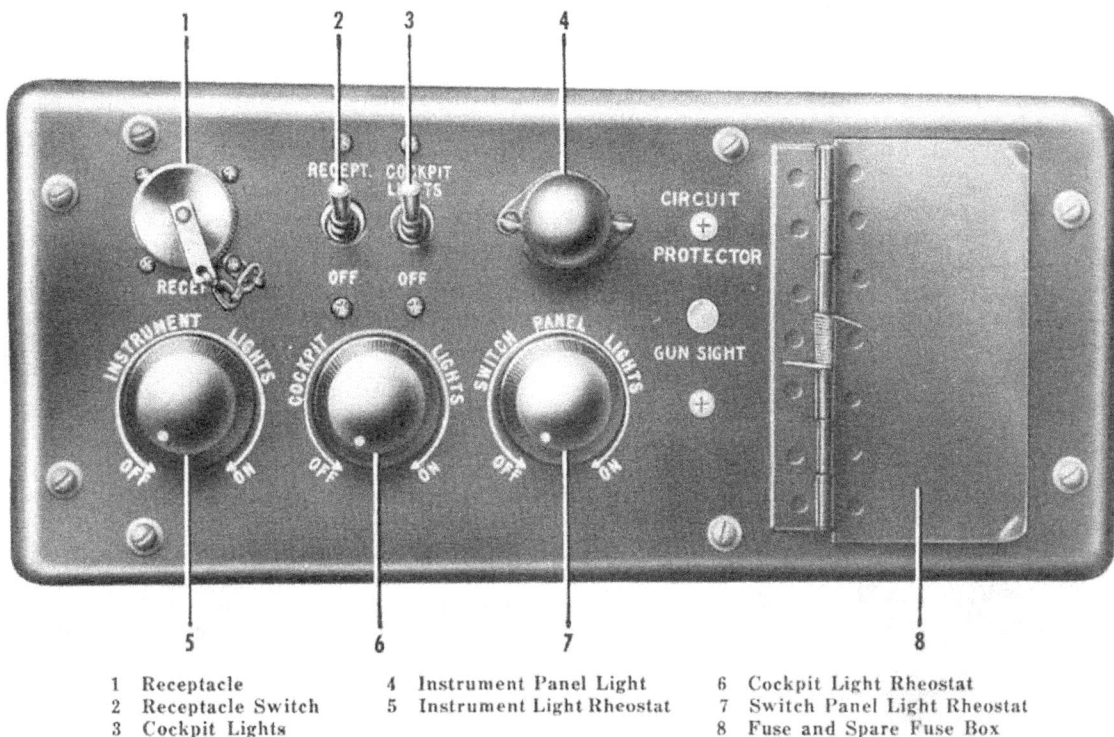

1 Receptacle
2 Receptacle Switch
3 Cockpit Lights
4 Instrument Panel Light
5 Instrument Light Rheostat
6 Cockpit Light Rheostat
7 Switch Panel Light Rheostat
8 Fuse and Spare Fuse Box

Figure 15—Gunner's Electrical Distribution Panel

for instrument, compartment, and distribution panel rheostats; compartment light switch; and receptacles and power switches.

(3) A light is installed on each side of both the pilot's cockpit and the gunner's compartment. The lights can be adjusted for direction and type of illumination.

w. RADIO EQUIPMENT. — The radio equipment consists of an AN/ARC-5 multiple-channel communication radio, a navigation receiver, an ARB receiver, a tactical radio (radar), an identification radio, and an interphone system. The radio master switch (Figure 14, Item 34) must be turned "ON" for all radio operations.

(1) **PILOT'S RADIO EQUIPMENT.**

(a) **AN/ARC-5 COMMUNICATION RADIO.**—The AN/ARC-5 communication radio consists of a transmitter control box, a receiver control box, and a jack box in the pilot's cockpit, and an operator's control box in the gunner's compartment.

1. **TRANSMITTER CONTROL BOX (Figure 16).**

a. The transmitter control box is on the right side of the pilot's cockpit, below the receiver control box. It contains seven buttons. The top four buttons select channels for the VHF transmitter and receiver simultaneously. The first button on the second row is an OFF switch which throws off all power to the transmitting equipment. The next two buttons select the two MHF transmitters, which have preset frequencies. Only one transmitter or channel may be selected at a time. The emission switch sends on "TONE," "CW," or "VOICE." The microphone switch or throttle switch keys the transmitters.

b. **To transmit,** turn the battery switch on; make certain that all circuit breaker buttons are pushed in; select the desired transmitter (allow 15 seconds' warm-up); set the emission switch for "TONE," "CW," or "VOICE"; depress the "push-to-talk" button on the hand microphone or throttle if on "VOICE."

NOTE

To reduce battery drain and increase dynamotor life, place the transmitter emission switch in "VOICE" unless continued use in "CW" or "TONE" is expected. In "CW" and "TONE," the dynamotor is constantly running; in "VOICE," the dynamotor starts and stops with each keying. Keying in "VOICE" therefore involves a heavy starting current which reduces the life of the dynamotor and should be avoided.

c. If sending on the VHF transmitter, select the desired channel with one of the top four buttons. If sending on an MHF transmitter, reception will be on the frequency of the last VHF button pressed previous to the selection of the

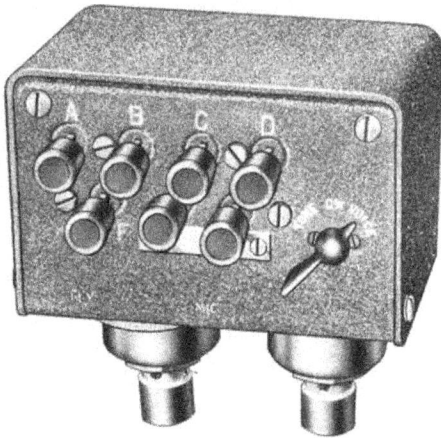

Figure 16—Communication Radio Transmitter Control Box

transmitter. To change receivers, again depress a VHF button before returning to the desired transmitter.

CAUTION

After pressing any of the four top buttons, wait six seconds before pressing either the second or the third button from the left on the bottom row; otherwise, overheating of the band selector motor may result.

2. **RECEIVER CONTROL BOX** (Figure 17).

a. The receiver control box is on the right side of the pilot's cockpit and controls three receivers. Receiver A is the VHF receiver which operates on one of four channels selected by the VHF buttons on the transmitter control box. Receiver B is the ARB (MHF) receiver which receives on a preset frequency. Receiver C is the ARC-HF receiver which also receives on a preset

frequency. A limited range sensitivity control is installed above each receiver switch. Moving the control in the direction of the arrow increases sensitivity but also increases noise interference. The control should be set for maximum tolerable noise in order to gain maximum sensitivity.

b. The volume control is on the lower left side of the receiver control box and controls the audio for all sets.

c. The microphone selector switch is on the upper left side of the receiver control box and selects "I.C.S." or "RADIO."

d. **To receive,** turn the battery switch on; check the circuit breakers; release the "push-to-talk" button; select the desired receiver by means of one of the three switches (if using the VHF receiver, select one of the four channels on the transmitter control box); adjust the sensitivity controls for maximum tolerable noise with the other receivers off; adjust the volume control; turn the microphone selector switch to "RADIO"; release the microphone switch or the throttle switch.

NOTE

All three receivers, plus the navigation receiver, can be operated at the same time. Under normal conditions, all of them will be switched on unless specific orders to the contrary are given.

Figure 17—Communication Radio Receiver Control Box

3. **JACK BOX (Figure 18).** — The jack box has two jacks on top, one for the hand microphone and one for the extension to the pilot's head set. The extension cable on the side of the jack box is for the connection of the oxygen mask microphone. The lower plug in the side of the box is connected to the throttle switch. This

Figure 18—Pilot's Jack Box

switch pulls in the transmitter selected and switches the antenna relay from the receiver to the transmitter. When the hand microphone is used, the same result is obtained by depressing the microphone switch. Use the throttle switch when the mask microphone is being used.

(b) AN/ARR-2 NAVIGATION RECEIVER.

1. The AN/ARR-2 navigation receiver is installed in the airplane for homing purposes.

2. The navigation receiver controls are on the right side of the receiver switch box (Figure 16). The controls consist of a crank which selects one of six bands, a window which shows the number of the selected band, a sensitivity switch which also acts as an on-off switch, a pitch control which also corrects for any tuning error, and a CW-VOICE control.

NOTE

The sensitivity control should be adjusted to produce a usable weak signal, or, if the desired signal cannot be heard, a fairly strong background hiss. If the signal is too strong, a clear-cut course indication cannot be obtained.

3. **To operate the receiver,** plug in the head set; turn the receiver on; select the correct band; turn to "CW" (or "VOICE"); adjust the pitch for a pleasing tone and correct for error in reception; adjust for sensitivity; listen for signal.

(c) ARB FERRY RADIO. — The ARB control box (Figure 19) is installed in the airplane for ferry purposes only and is removed when the airplane is made ready for combat duty. The controls consist of a tuning head (Figure 20) and a

control box aft of the receiver and transmitter control boxes on the right side of the cockpit.

1. The INCREASE OUTPUT control is a sensitivity control and acts as a "gain" control when the airplane is flown on the radio range.

2. The frequency band control selects one of six bands.

3. The M.V.C.-A.V.C. control permits continuous wave (C.W.) reception or modulated continuous wave (M.C.W.) reception in the manual volume control ("M.V.C.") position. The automatic volume control ("A.V.C.") position provides for reception of M.C.W. signals utilizing the A.V.C. circuits and normal selectivity in the "SHARP" position. The "BROAD" position is used when M.C.W. signals are being located on the two higher frequency bands; it also acts as an on-off switch.

4. **To operate the ferry radio,** plug into the receiver box; turn the M.V.C.-A.V.C. control from "OFF" to the desired position; turn the frequency band control to the desired band; tune with the tuning-head control; regulate sensitivity with the INCREASE OUTPUT control.

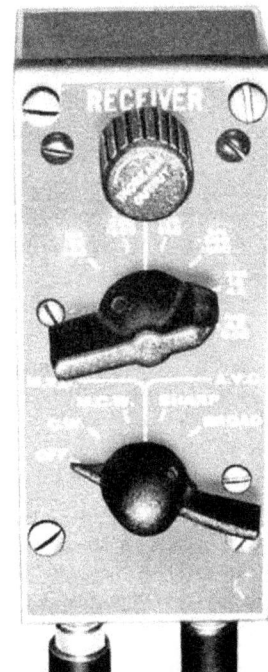

Figure 19—ARB Ferry Radio Control Box

Figure 20—ARB Radio Tuning Head

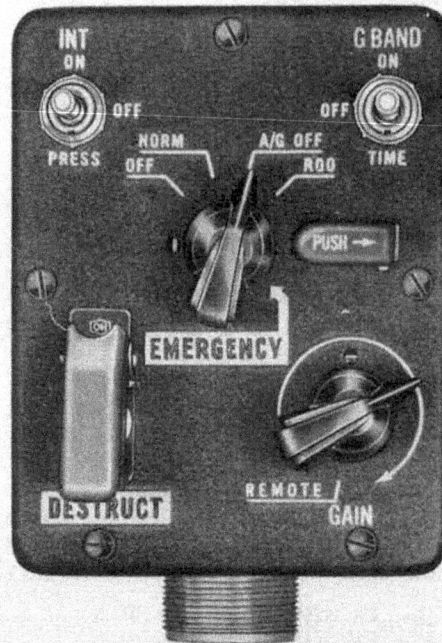

Figure 21—Pilot's Identification Radio Control Box

5. **To receive M.C.W. signals,** operate the M.V.C.-A.V.C. control to the "M.C.W." position; set the frequency band control to a position corresponding to the frequency range and type of antenna desired. Tune the signal for maximum output. If automatic volume control is desired, reset the M.V.C.-A.V.C. control to the desired position under A.V.C. and readjust the volume control for the desired output level.

6. **To receive C.W. signals,** operate the M.V.C.-A.V.C. control to the "C.W." position; set the frequency band control to the desired frequency band.

7. When operating on **radio range,** the M.V.C.-A.V.C. control will automatically be on the "M.V.C." position. Use the INCREASE OUTPUT control as a "gain" control. It is necessary to be on radio range in order to obtain course indications.

8. When the M.V.C.-A.V.C. control is on "SHARP" or "BROAD," the INCREASE OUTPUT control can be used on any of the communication channels.

(d) **IDENTIFICATION RADIO.** — This equipment has two control boxes: one in the

pilot's cockpit (Figure 21) and one in the gunner's compartment. The control box in the pilot's cockpit is just forward of the map case.

(e) **INTERPHONE SYSTEM.** — The interphone system is regulated as follows:

1. Turn the battery switch (Figure 14, Item 5) to the "BATTERY" position.

2. Place the selector switch, in the upper left corner of the receiver control box, in the "I.C.S." position.

CAUTION

Be careful not to go on the air accidentally. Make certain of the position of the microphone selector switch; "I.C.S." is for interphone: "RADIO" is for radio transmission. Accidental radio transmission may give your position away to the enemy.

3. When using the microphone, depress the microphone switch to talk; when using the throat microphone, depress the throttle switch (Figure 6, Item 15). Release the switch to listen.

4. The volume control has no effect on the interphone.

NOTE

When the interphone system is being used, radio signals can be heard as a background.

(2) GUNNER'S RADIO EQUIPMENT.

(a) **COMMUNICATION RADIO CONTROL BOX (Figure 22).** — The communication radio control box is on the right forward side of the gunner's compartment. It contains a volume control and an I.C.S.-RADIO switch. The volume control has no effect on the interphone. When the selector switch is in the "I.C.S." position, the gunner may communicate with the pilot. When the selector switch is in "RADIO," the gunner can transmit and receive according to the pilot's selection. The gunner should make certain that the controls are set for "C.W." or "TONE" if he wishes to transmit by key. When he is through transmitting, he should notify the pilot to switch back to "VOICE." The forward key (Figure 30, Item 2) is just above the control box; the aft key (Figure 31, Item 3) is in the aft left corner of the compartment. The circuit breaker junction box (Figure 30, Item 4) is just forward of the gunner's control box.

Figure 22—Gunner's Radio Control Box

(b) **RADAR.** — The radar (tactical radio) indicator is on the forward center deck of the gunner's compartment. The control box (Figure 31, Item 9) and the hydraulic controls (Figure 31, Item 10) for operating the antennas are below the throttle control.

(c) **IDENTIFICATION RADIO CONTROL BOX.** — The gunner's radio control box is on the left side of the gunner's compartment. To destroy the receiver unit, operate the firing switch.

(d) **INTERPHONE SYSTEM.** — The interphone system is regulated as follows:

1. Turn the selector switch on the control box to the "I.C.S." position.

2. Plug in the mike jack at the bottom of the control box.

3. Depress the microphone switch (Figure 30, Item 1).

NOTE

When the gunner is in position to fire the guns, he can use the switch (Figure 26, Item 1) on the left (facing aft) gun spade grip.

5. USEFUL LOAD INSTALLATION CONTROLS.

The following armament controls are installed in the Model SBD-6 Airplane: bombing controls in the pilot's cockpit; fixed gun controls in the pilot's cockpit; flexible gun controls in the gunner's compartment; gun cameras for the fixed and flexible guns; and smoke tank controls, signal pistol, and night drift signals in the gunner's compartment.

a. ELECTRICAL BOMBING CONTROLS.

(1) The three bomb racks are armed from the electrical distribution panel as follows: Place the battery switch (Figure 14, Item 5) or the battery and generator (Figure 14, Item 4) switches in the "ON" position; place the master armament switch (Figure 14, Item 15) in the "ON" position; set the nose-arming switch (Figure 14,

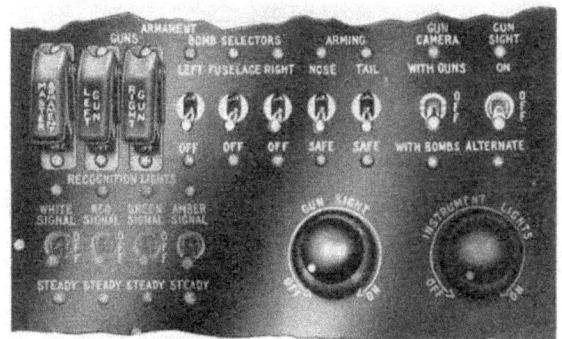

Figure 23—Armament Switches

Item 25), tail-arming switch (Figure 14, Item 24) or both, in the "ON" position.

(2) To release the bombs, place the right fuselage, or left bomb selector switches (Figure 14, Items 10, 11, and 12) in the "ON" position; depress the button on top of the control stick (Figure 6, Item 20).

NOTE

To drop the three bombs simultaneously, place the three bomb selector switches in the "ON" position.

b. MANUAL BOMBING CONTROLS.

(1) For manual bombing operations, the bombs can be electrically armed from the electrical distribution panel as noted under "Electrical Bombing Controls," above, or they can be manually armed by means of the manual arming control (Figure 6, Item 21) on the bottom of the manual bomb release quadrant (Figure 24). To arm the tail fuse only, move the handle forward four notches only. To arm both the nose fuses and the tail fuses, move the control all of the way to "ARMED."

Figure 24—Manual Bomb Release Quadrant

(2) To release the bombs, move the selector lever on the bomb control quadrant (Figure 6, Item 19) to the "R." (right), "L." (left), or "SALVO" (center) position.

NOTE

To release the three bombs simultaneously, place the selector lever in the

"SALVO" position. However, if the bombs are to be released individually, place the selector lever in the "L." and "R." positions before placing it in "SALVO."

c. FIXED GUN CONTROLS.

(1) Two Browning, .50-caliber, fixed guns are installed in the pilot's cockpit.

(2) To prepare the guns for firing, the following switches on the electrical distribution panel must be placed in the "ON" position: the battery switch (Figure 14, Item 5) or the battery and generator (Figure 14, Item 4) switches; the master armament switch (Figure 14, Item 15); the left, right, or both gun selector switches (Figure 14, Items 13 and 14).

(3) To fire the guns, grip the trigger switch on the forward side of the control stick.

(4) The illuminated gun sight (Figure 10) is installed on the vertical centerline of the airplane, beneath the compass, and is operated as follows: Adjust the pilot's seat for height; place the master armament switch in the "ON" position; place the gun sight switch (Figure 14, Item 22) in the "ON" position; adjust the rheostat knob (Figure 14, Item 27) on the electrical distribution panel for the desired intensity. Glare is eliminated from the gun sight by means of a smoked-glass lens.

d. FLEXIBLE GUN CONTROLS.

(1) The Browning, .30-caliber, twin flexible guns are in the aft section of the gunner's compartment. The button (Figure 26, Item 5) incorporated on top of the right (facing aft) gun spade grip operates the gun camera; the button (Figure 26, Item 1) on top of the left gun spade grip operates the gunner's throat microphone.

(2) To prepare the guns for firing:

(a) Move the forward and aft sections of the enclosure under the center section enclosure.

(b) Push back the panels on each side of the gun tunnel doors.

(c) Depress the pedal (Figure 31, Item 7), located directly below the right foot brace, to open the gun tunnel doors and release the stowage latch.

(d) Grasp the gun adapter spade grips and pull the gun back until it automatically locks in place.

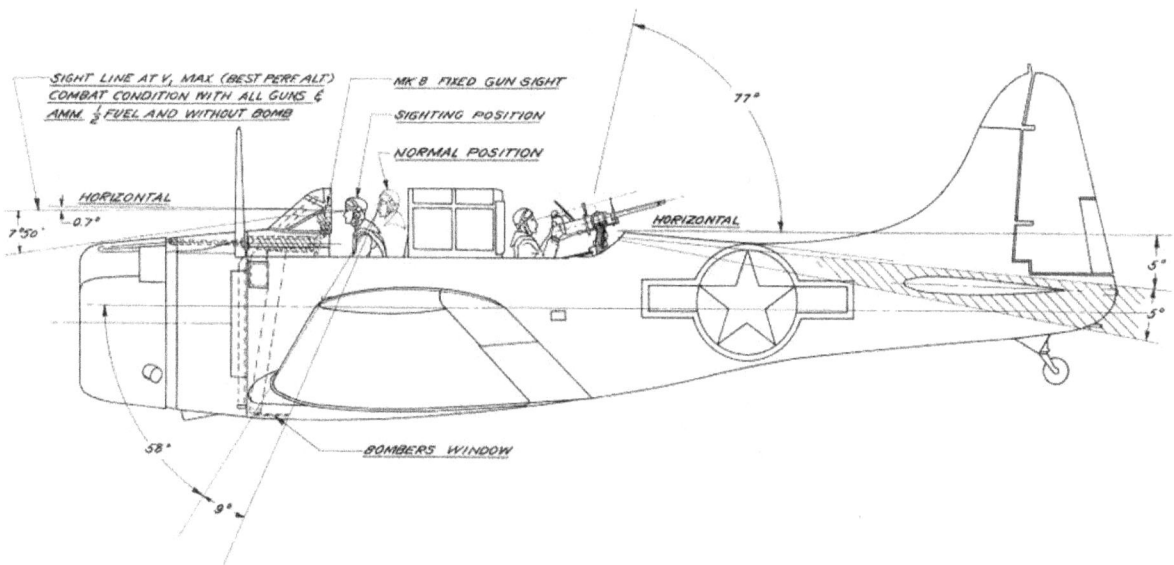

Figure 25—Pilot's Vision and Flexible Gun Range

(e) Raise the bead-and-ring sights into position.

(f) Depress the handle (Figure 26, Item 4) in the center of the gun truck to permit the adapter to swivel on the gun ring.

(g) To tilt the seat and guns, depress the lever (Figure 32, Item 3) immediately aft of the right foot brace.

(h) Charge the guns by pulling back the handle (Figure 27, Item 4) on the outboard side of each gun.

(3) An illuminated gun sight (Figure 27, Item 1) is installed on the aft end of the gun adapter and is controlled by the rheostat knob (Figure 27, Item 2) directly below the sight.

(4) To fire the guns, set the safety lever, between the trigger levers, in the "FIRE" position; then grasp the gun spade grips and push the trigger levers (Figure 26, Item 2) with thumb pressure (either lever fires both guns).

(5) To stow the guns:

(a) Set the safety lever in the "SAFE" position.

(b) Place the gun truck in a center position.

(c) Latch the ring-and-bead sights in a stowed position.

(d) Depress the pedal (Figure 31, Item 7), located directly below the right foot brace, to open the gun tunnel doors.

(e) Depress or lift the small lever on the top center of the gun truck, and push the guns aft into the tunnel.

(f) Lock the guns in position.

(g) Return the panels on each side of the gun tunnel doors to their normal position.

e. GUN CAMERAS.

(1) The **fixed gun camera** is mounted on the leading edge of the right outer wing bomb rack and is regulated from the electrical distribution panel as follows: place the battery switch (Figure 14, Item 5) or the battery and generator (Figure 14, Item 4) switches in the "ON" position; place the master armament switch (Figure 14, Item 15) in the "ON" position; place the gun camera switch (Figure 14, Item 23) in the "WITH GUNS" position. When the trigger switch is gripped or the bomb release button is depressed, the camera will operate.

NOTE

To operate the camera without firing the guns or dropping the bombs, leave the gun and bomb switches in the "OFF" position.

1 Interphone (Throat Microphone) Switch   3 Gun Adapter Release Lever   5 Gun Camera Switch
2 Gun Trigger Levers   4 Gun Adapter Handle   6 Shoulder Armor Plate

Figure 26—Flexible Guns—Stowed Position

1 Illuminated Gun Sight   3 Gun Camera Switch
2 Gun Sight Rheostat   4 Gun Charger Control

Figure 27—Flexible Guns—Firing Position

(2) The **flexible gun camera** is mounted on top of the right gun and is operated as follows: Turn on the camera switch (Figure 32, Item 1) located to the left of the gunner when he is firing aft. and depress the button (Figure 26, Item 5) on top of the right gun spade grip.

NOTE

When the camera is mounted, it renders the right gun inoperative and prevents stowage of the guns.

f. SMOKE TANK CONTROLS.

(1) The smoke tank controls consist of the tail pipe control (Figure 31, Item 4), the gate valve (Figure 31, Item 6), and the CO_2 bottle (Figure 31, Item 5) which is located on the aft left side of the compartment.

(2) To operate the smoke tank, lower the tail pipe control so that the chemical flows away from the airplane; open the valve on the CO_2 bottle to build up pressure in the smoke tank; and raise the gate valve handle so that the chemical flows into the atmosphere.

(3) To close the smoke tank, depress the gate valve handle, raise the tail pipe control handle to the retracted position, and turn off the CO_2 valve handle.

NOTE

It is not necessary for the CO_2 valve handle to be turned off if the gunner wishes to repeat the operation.

(4) In an emergency, it is possible to jettison the smoke tank by operating the electrical or manual bomb release. (See paragraph **5.a.** and **b.**, above.)

g. AN-M8 SIGNAL PISTOL (Figure 31, Item 1). — The AN-M8 signal pistol is on the aft left side of the gunner's compartment and is rigidly mounted to the structure. Twelve cartridges are located forward of the pistol in canvas containers (Figure 31, Item 2). To install a cartridge, break open the pistol.

h. FLOAT LIGHTS. — The five float lights (night drift signals) are aft of the flexible gun ammunition box. These lights are principally used at night to check drift variations, but can also be used during daylight. The gunner computes the amount of drift by means of the smoke, or smoky light, which is released when the float strikes the water.

6. MISCELLANEOUS EQUIPMENT.

The miscellaneous equipment installed in the airplane consists of the life raft, pilot's chartboard, starter crank, emergency rations and fresh water, map and instrument cases, and relief tubes. A baggage compartment is also provided.

a. LIFE RAFT.

(1) The Type D life raft is stowed in a compartment in the aft left side of the fuselage. A latch on the outside of the compartment provides ready access to the raft.

(2) The raft incorporates a handle which is pulled to allow CO_2 gas to inflate the raft. However, this handle is only for inflating the raft and should not be used to lift it. If the raft fails to inflate when the handle is pulled, the raft can be inflated by means of the mouth.

b. CHARTBOARD (Figure 33, Item 6).

(1) The pilot's chartboard is used for navigation calculations and is stowed under the instrument panel. To slide the chartboard from the stowed position, release the latch on the left side of the board.

(2) The chartboard is fitted with a filing space below the hinged cover. This space is suitable for standard-sized index cards, computers, pencils, etc. The top of the cover is fitted with retainers in each corner to secure the standard aircraft navigational plotting board. Data sheets may be glued, or otherwise secured, to the index side of the hinged cover.

c. BAGGAGE COMPARTMENT.—The door of the baggage compartment is on the right side of the fuselage and is locked by a Sesame combination lock which is set to the last three numbers of the manufacturer's serial number. The name plate showing this combination is found on the right side of the overturn structure behind the pilot's head. The radar equipment is installed in the forward portion of the compartment, just beneath the tubular-shaped compartment of the life raft.

d. STARTER CRANK. — The crank for energizing the engine starter is stowed in the baggage compartment.

e. EMERGENCY RATIONS AND FRESH WATER. — Emergency rations and fresh water are stowed in a bag attached to the life raft. An additional water canteen of one-quart capacity is stowed in the pilot's cockpit and in the gunner's compartment.

f. MAP AND INSTRUMENT CASE.—A canvas map case (Figure 6, Item 1) is secured to the fuselage on the left side of the pilot's seat. In the front of the case are two additional compartments

for pencils and calculating equipment. The gunner's data case (Figure 32, Item 2) is secured to the aft wall of the compartment, on the right side.

g. RELIEF TUBES. — The pilot's relief tube is underneath the seat on the right side. The gunner's relief tube is on the right side of the compartment, at floor level.

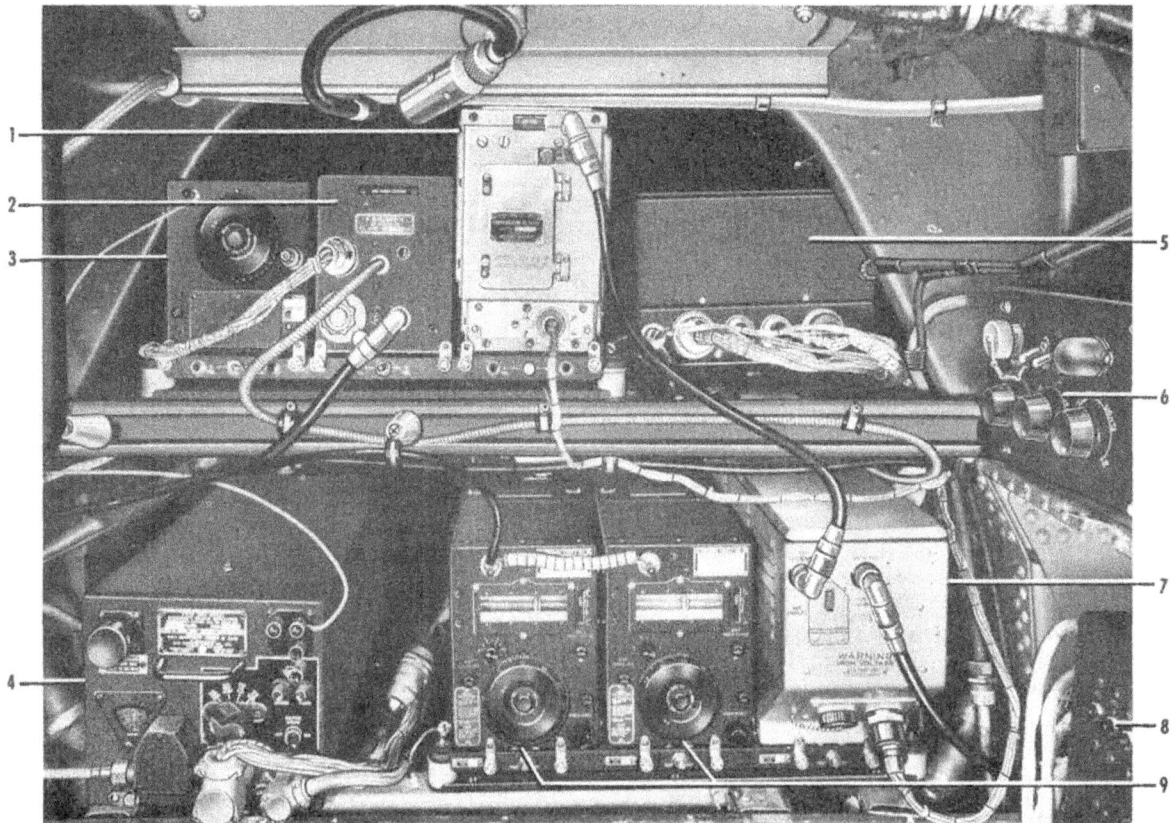

1	VHF Receiver	6	Electrical Distribution Panel
2	Navigation Receiver	7	VHF Transmitter
3	HF Receiver	8	Junction Box
4	ARB Receiver	9	MHF Transmitters
5	Modulator		

Figure 28—Gunner's Compartment—Front

1   Left Armor Plate Locking Pin
2   Seat Swivel Locking Pin
3   Safety Belt
4   Seat Height Adjustment Lever
5   Right Armor Plate Locking Pin
6   Chest Armor Plates

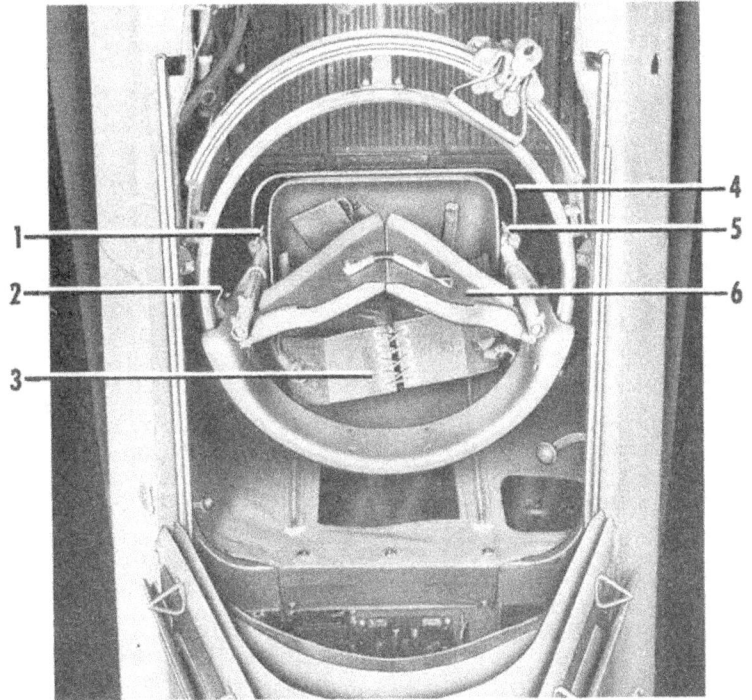

1   Microphone Switch
2   Transmitter Key (forward position)
3   Communication Radio Control Box
4   Junction Box
5   Interphone Amplifier
6   Rudder Pedal
7   Rudder Pedal Adjustment

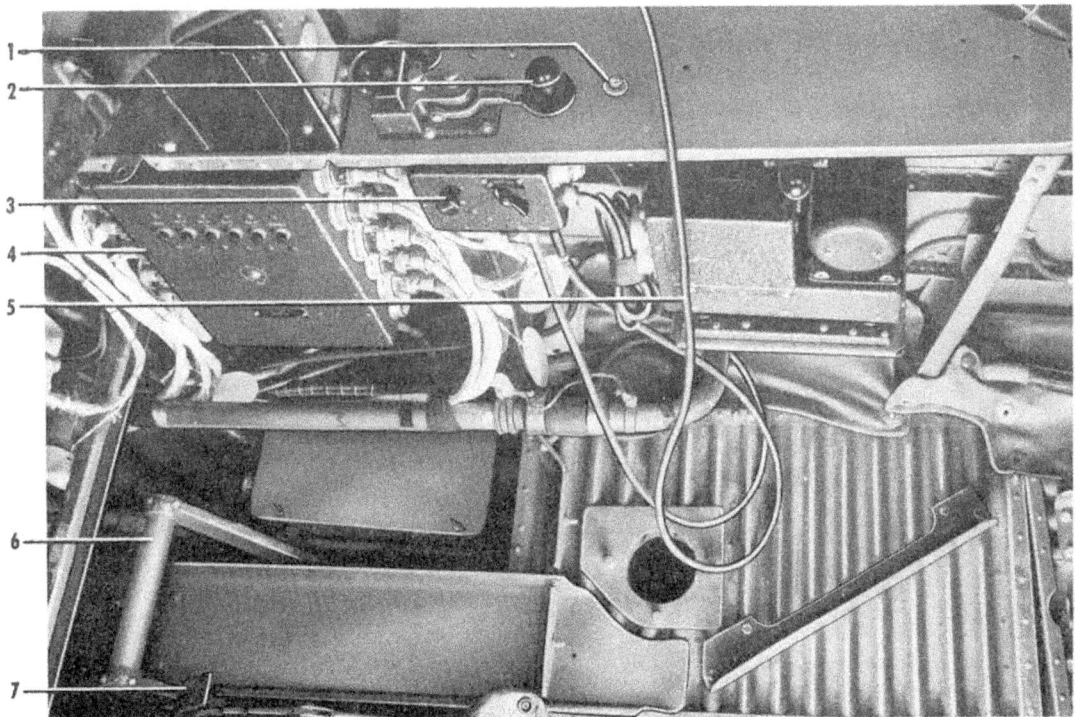

Figure 29—Gunner's Compartment—Top

Figure 30—Gunner's Compartment—Right Side

1	Cut-out for AN-M8 Signal Pistol	5	CO₂ Bottle
2	Signal Flare Cartridge Containers	6	Gate Valve Control
3	Transmitter Key (aft position)	7	Gun Tunnel Door Control Lever
4	Tail Pipe Control		

1 Cut-out for AN-M8 Signal Pistol   5 CO_2 Bottle   8 Throttle Control
2 Signal Flare Cartridge Containers   6 Gate Valve Control   9 Radar Control Box
3 Transmitter Key (aft position)   7 Gun Tunnel Door Control Lever 10 Radar Controls
4 Tail Pipe Control   11 Control Stick (stowed position)

Figure 31—Gunner's Compartment—Left Side

1 Gun Camera Switch Box   3 Seat Tilt Control
2 Data Case   4 CO_2 Bottle

Figure 32—Gunner's Compartment—Rear

SECTION II
POWER PLANT

1. ENGINE.

The Model SBD-6 Airplane is powered by a Wright Cyclone, model R-1820-66, nine-cylinder, radial, air-cooled engine which is geared three to two and is equipped with a two-speed supercharger and a Stromberg injection carburetor, model PD12-K10.

a. ENGINE RATING.

	BHP	RPM	BLOWER	ALTITUDE (no ram)
Normal	1200	2500	LOW	S.L.—2,700
	900	2500	HIGH	17,500
Military	1300	2600	LOW	S.L.—1,500
(30 min.)	1000	2600	HIGH	14,700
Take-off	1300	2600	LOW	S.L.

WARNING

During the first 10 hours of flight operation engine power shall be held to the minimum required for safe operation of the airplane. High BMEP and excessively lean mixture should be avoided. These instructions are not to be construed to prohibit such operation at rated power as may be necessary for checking during production acceptance tests, but such operations shall be held to the minimum practicable.

b. FUEL.—Grade 100/130, Spec. AN-F-28.

c. OIL.—Grade 1120, Spec. AN-VV-O-446a.

d. MAXIMUM DIVING RPM.—3100 rpm for 30 seconds (do all diving in "LOW" blower ratio).

e. PROPELLER.—The airplane is equipped with a Hamilton Standard, three-bladed, hydromatic, constant-speed propeller, 10 feet 10 inches in diameter (hub 33D50; blades 6511A-9). The positive low-pitch setting is 18½ degrees; the positive high-pitch setting is 48½ degrees.

f. STARTER AND PRIMER.

(1) The airplane is equipped with an Eclipse, type 436, hand inertia starter. The starter crank is stowed on the floor of the baggage compartment; the crank socket is on the right side of the cowling. The starter control (Figure 2, Item 15) is immediately above the electrical distribution panel in the cockpit. To engage the starter, pull out the control handle and hold it until the engine starts and is running smoothly (THE BOOSTER COIL IS OPERATED BY THE STARTER CONTROL); then release the handle and push it in. Do not engage the starter until the cranking speed is approximately 78 rpm.

(2) The engine primer switch (Figure 14, Item 3) is in the upper left corner of the electrical distribution panel. The electric auxiliary fuel pump must be used to supply pressure for priming before the engine is started.

g. PROPELLER GOVERNOR CONTROL (Figure 6, Item 3).

(1) The propeller governor control is on the aft side of the engine quadrant. Move the control "DOWN" to increase rpm; move the control "UP" to decrease rpm. Full "DOWN" position should result in take-off rpm. Finer adjustment can be obtained by rotating the knob on the side of the control lever. Turn the knob counterclockwise to increase rpm.

(2) An hydraulic accumulator is connected to the propeller oil system to provide a reserve supply of oil to the governor at sufficient pressure to change the propeller pitch when the regular supply is interrupted for any reason. The accumulator pressure should be checked each day prior to flight. The pressure should be 175 psi when the engine is not running.

h. MIXTURE CONTROL (Figure 6, Item 18).

(1) This engine is equipped with a PD12-K10 Bendix-Stromberg injection carburetor. The mixture control has three positions: "AUTO RICH," "AUTO LEAN," and "IDLE CUT-OFF." Fuel will be discharged from the carburetor at any fuel pressure above five psi when the mixture control is not in the "IDLE CUT-OFF" position. To prevent flooding through inadvertent use of the auxiliary fuel pump, the mixture control shall always be left in "IDLE CUT-OFF" when the engine is not running.

(2) For all ground operations, take-offs, and landings, the mixture control shall be set in "AUTO RICH." For all other flight operations, it is permissible to use "AUTO LEAN." Satisfactory, continuous operation in "AUTO LEAN" above 65

1 Tachometer
2 Altimeter
3 Directional Gyro
4 Engine Gage Unit
5 Airspeed Indicator
6 Chartboard
7 Clock
8 Cylinder Head Temperature Indicator
9 Manifold Pressure Gage
10 Bank-and-Climb Gyro
11 Turn-and-Bank Indicator
12 Rate-of-Climb Indicator
13 Outside Air Temperature Indicator
14 Fuel Quantity Indicator
15 Automatic Pilot Oil Pressure Gage

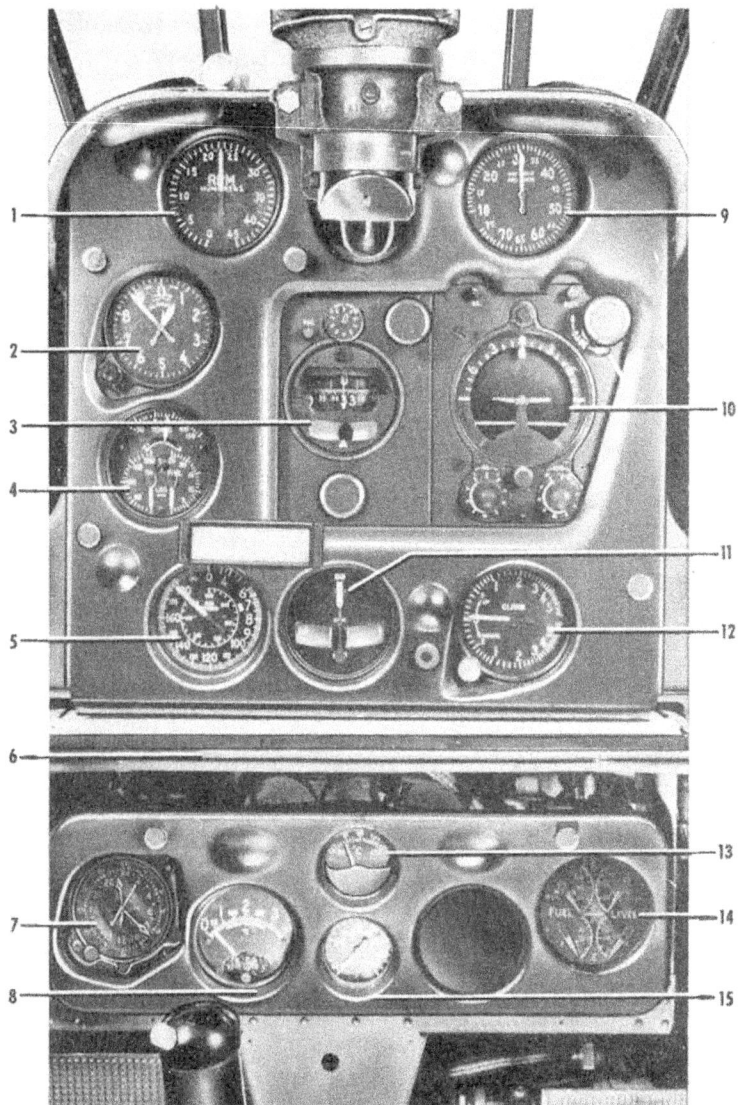

Figure 33—Pilot's Instrument Panel

percent power is absolutely contingent upon not exceeding cylinder head temperature limits.

(3) When selecting different mixture settings, always feel for the notch which indicates proper positioning of the control lever on the carburetor. Backlash may cause the correct positions to differ slightly from the markings on the control quadrant.

(4) The rpm-manifold-pressure relationships specified in the "Operating Limits Chart" shall not be exceeded.

i. SUPERCHARGER (BLOWER) CONTROL (Figure 6, Item 12).

(1) The blower control lever (black knob) controls the two-speed supercharger ("HIGH" and "LOW" blower) which forces more fuel-air mixture into the cylinders. Higher altitude power rating is obtained by using the supercharger.

CAUTION

"LOW" blower is to be used for all take-offs and landings.

(2) Do not, except in an emergency, shift the supercharger control oftener than at five-minute intervals, since overheating may result. The control must be at the extremity of its travel ("HIGH" or "LOW") at all times to prevent clutch slippage and insure available rated power. The supercharger is equipped with a roller-type clutch. The clutch should be shifted to "HIGH" blower each flight day in order to disludge the clutch. This type of clutch will sludge up if the daily shift is not made.

(3) To change from "LOW" to "HIGH" ratio:

(a) Place the mixture control in "AUTO RICH."

(b) Close the throttle, as necessary, to avoid exceeding the desired manifold pressure in "HIGH" ratio.

(c) Reduce rpm, if practicable (not below 1700 rpm).

(d) Shift rapidly from "LOW" to "HIGH."

(e) Readjust rpm, throttle setting, and mixture control to obtain desired power.

(4) To change from "HIGH" to "LOW" ratio:

(a) Shift rapidly from "HIGH" to "LOW."

(b) Adjust power and mixture as necessary.

j. **CARBURETOR AIR CONTROL (Figure 2, Item 14).**

(1) When the carburetor air control is in the "DIRECT" position, carburetor air is taken under full ram from a scoop at the front of the engine cowling; when this control is in the "ALTERNATE" position, carburetor air is taken from a protected source within the engine cowling.
"DIRECT"...........................FULL IN
"ALTERNATE" FULL OUT (¼ turn; then pull)

(2) The carburetor air control shall be in the "DIRECT" position for take-offs, dives, and landings and for normal operation; however, during heavy rain, snow, sleet, icing conditions, or inadvertent clogging of the external air intake, the alternate position should be used.

NOTE

This control must always be in either the full "DIRECT" or full "ALTERNATE" position at all times.

k. **CARBURETOR AIR FILTER CONTROL (Figure 2, Item 7).**—Provision is made for the installation of a carburetor air filter and a special direct air intake duct. The carburetor air filter control, when installed, is directly above the oil cooler scoop control. For filtered air, pull the control **out.** THE CARBURETOR AIR CONTROL MUST BE IN THE "DIRECT" POSITION BEFORE THE FILTER CAN BE USED.

l. **COWL FLAP CONTROL (Figure 2, Item 4).**

(1) The cowl flap control is located at the left of the lower instrument panel.

(2) **To open the cowl flaps,** move the selector control to the "OPEN" position; depress the engine pump control handle (Figure 7, Item 6), or operate the hydraulic hand pump (Figure 5, Item 4) until the cowl flaps are in the desired position; then return the selector control to "NEUTRAL."

(3) **To close the cowl flaps,** move the selector control to the "CLOSED" position; depress the engine pump control handle, or operate the hydraulic hand pump until the cowl flaps are "CLOSED"; then return the selector control to "NEUTRAL."

(4) The cowl flaps shall be adjusted so that the following cylinder head temperatures will not be exceeded:

Take-off ....248°C   (478°F) (5 min)
Military Power ......232°C   (450°F) (30 min)
Normal Rated Power 232°C   (450°F) (1 hour)
Normal Rated Power 218°C   (424°F) (cont)
70% Normal Rated
   Power and Below..205°C   (401°F) (cont)

m. **CHANGING POWER CONDITIONS.** — When changing power, always follow the procedure outlined below to prevent excessive pressures within the cylinders.

(1) To increase engine power:

(a) Adjust the mixture control for the power condition specified in the "Specific Engine Flight Chart" (Figure 36).

(b) Adjust the propeller control for the desired rpm.

(c) Adjust the throttle for the desired manifold pressure.

(2) To decrease engine power:

(a) Adjust the throttle for approximate desired manifold pressure.

(b) Adjust the propeller control for the desired rpm.

(c) Adjust the mixture control for the power condition specified in the "Specific Engine Flight Chart" (Figure 36).

(d) Readjust the throttle, if necessary.

2. FUEL SYSTEM.

The fuel system incorporates two main fuel tanks, two auxiliary fuel tanks, provision for two droppable fuel tanks. fuel tank selectors for the fixed fuel tank system and the droppable fuel tank system, a defueling valve, an auxiliary fuel pump, an engine-driven fuel pump, and an engine primer. (See diagram, Figure 34.)

The two main fuel tanks are in the wing center section, and the two auxiliary tanks are in the outer wings. These four tanks are self-sealing and the fuel capacities given below are for the tanks in their lined condition. A droppable fuel tank can be carried under each wing panel by utilizing the wing bomb racks. Approximate fuel tank capacities are as follows:

Fuel Tank	Capacity
RH Main	80 gal
LH Main	80 gal
RH Aux	70 gal
LH Aux	70 gal
RH Drop	58 gal
LH Drop	58 gal
Total	416 gal

There are no interconnections between the tanks and each tank has individual supply lines to the tank selector valves; therefore, each tank must be filled and drained separately.

a. FUEL TANK SELECTOR CONTROL (Figure 6, Item 5).—The main fuel tank selector control is installed forward of the trim tab controls and selects the tank from which fuel is to be withdrawn or shuts off the fuel supply to the engine-driven and auxiliary fuel pumps.

CAUTION

Do not take off, land, or dive with fuel supplied from the auxiliary fuel tanks. Use the auxiliary tanks for level flight only. Use the "L.H. MAIN" tank for take-offs.

b. DROPPABLE FUEL TANK SELECTOR CONTROL (Figure 6, Item 10). — The selector control for the droppable fuel tanks is below the fixed fuel tank selector, on the side of the control panel, and selects fuel from the droppable tanks. Select either the "L.H. DROP." or "R.H. DROP." before turning the main fuel tank selector control to "DROP. TANKS."

CAUTION

When the airplane is equipped with droppable tanks. it is recommended that the landing speed be increased from five to seven knots above normal.

c. DROPPABLE TANK RELEASE.—The droppable tanks are released by the electric or manual bomb selectors and the bomb release.

NOTE

When the droppable tanks are installed, only the center bomb rack can carry a bomb.

d. FUEL QUANTITY INDICATOR (Figure 33, Item 14).—The fuel quantity indicator is on the pilot's lower instrument panel and indicates in U.S. gallons the amount of fuel in the tanks during flight. The droppable tanks are not provided with an indicator.

e. FUEL PUMPS.

(1) The engine-driven fuel pump normally delivers fuel to the carburetor at a pressure of 16 to 18 psi (17 psi desired). The auxiliary fuel pump is operated by a switch (Figure 14, Item 2) on the upper left corner of the electrical distribution panel. The necessary pressure for starting and priming is supplied by the auxiliary fuel pump. As a precautionary measure against loss of fuel pressure, switch the auxiliary fuel pump on during take-offs, landings, and when changing tanks. If necessary, this pump can be used at high altitudes to aid in the prevention of vapor lock in the fuel system. When the engine is running and the auxiliary fuel pump is "ON," the pressure is 17.5 to 19.5 psi.

NOTE

Switch the auxiliary fuel pump on if the engine-driven pump fails during flight.

(2) If complete carburetor vapor trap failure occurs, as much as 28 gallons of fuel per hour may flow from the carburetor through the vapor return to the left main tank, and a normal flow

CARBURETOR

ENGINE-DRIVEN FUEL PUMP

DIAPHRAGM VENT LINE

DRAIN LINE

RH MAIN

LH MAIN

OFF

RH AUX

DROP TANKS

LH AUX

ENGINE-PRIMING VALVE

PRESSURE LINE

VENT LINE

STRAINER

FIRE WALL

DRAIN LINE

DIAPHRAGM VENT LINE

AUXILIARY FUEL PUMP

FUEL PRESSURE GAGE (ENGINE GAGE UNIT)

CARBURETOR VAPOR VENT LINE

MAIN SELECTOR VALVE

DEFUELING VALVE

DRAIN

LH SUMP SELECTOR FITTING

RH SUMP SELECTOR FITTING

LH AUX

LH MAIN

RH MAIN

RH AUX

VENT

VENT

FILLER WELL

FILLER WELL

SUMP

FINGER SCREEN

FINGER SCREEN

DROPPABLE TANK SELECTOR VALVE

SUMP

LH DROP 58 GALS

RH DROP 58 GALS

VENT OUTLET

VENT OUTLET

DISCONNECT FITTING

DISCONNECT FITTING

LH DROPPABLE FUEL TANK

RH DROPPABLE FUEL TANK

AIR PRESSURE

VENT

FUEL PRESSURE

FUEL SUPPLY

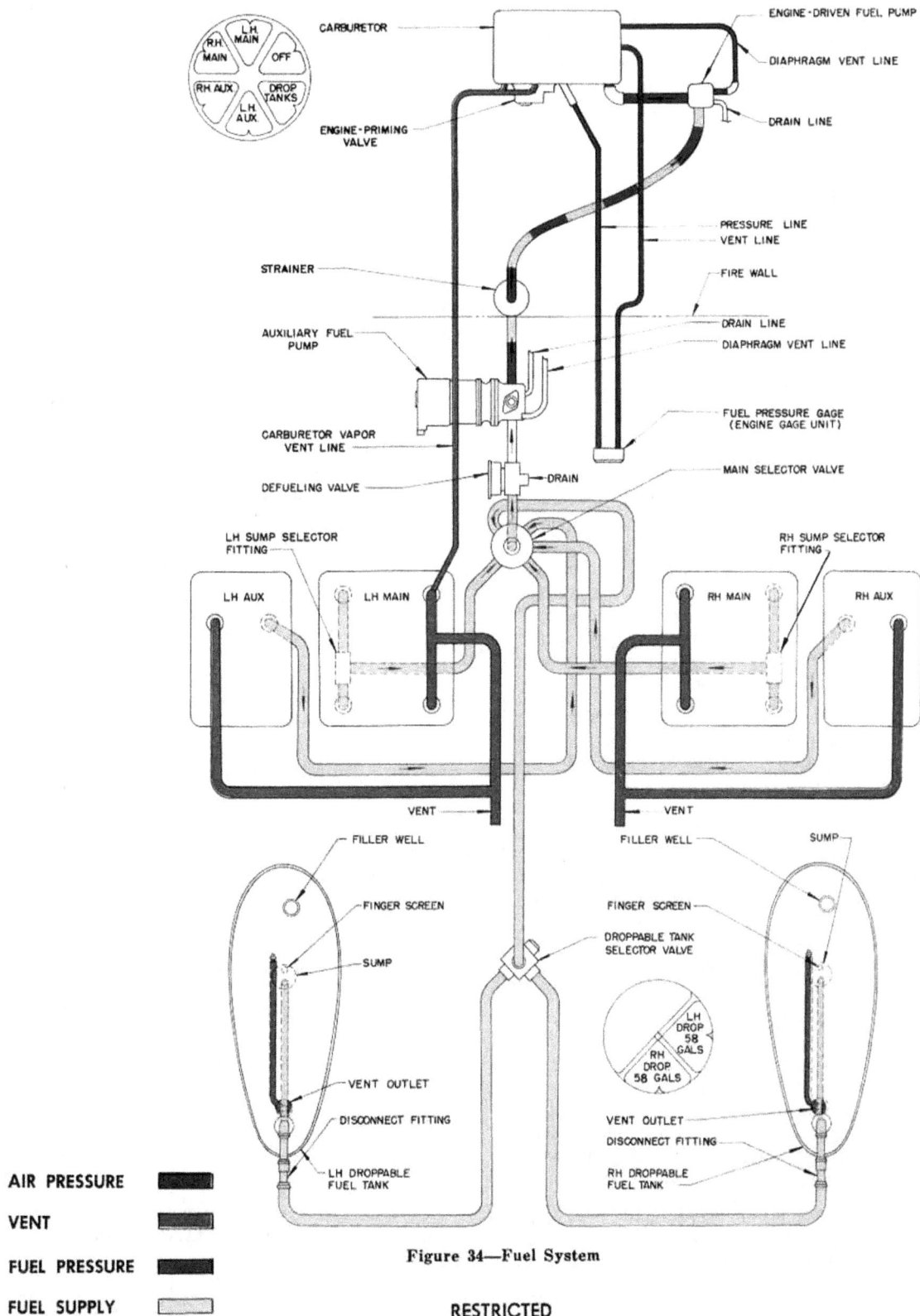

Figure 34—Fuel System

of as much as eight gallons per hour may be expected. Loss of fuel from the vent will result unless space has been provided by the **use of fuel from the left main tank during the initial stages of flight.**

3. OIL SYSTEM.

The oil system incorporates an oil tank, an oil cooler, a temperature control valve, and an oil check valve. (See diagram, Figure 35.)

The oil tank is directly forward of the fire wall and has a "with liner" capacity of 16.5 gallons with a three-gallon expansion space; the "without liner" capacity is 19.5 gallons with a three-gallon expansion space.

After the oil passes through the engine, it flows through an outlet to the rotary temperature control on the side of the oil cooler. The temperature control valve regulates the temperature of the oil being returned to the tank. At the control valve, cold oil is bypassed to the warm-up compartment in the bottom of the tank; warm oil is directed through the cooler muff to the top of the tank; hot oil is directed through the core of the cooler to the top of the tank. A check valve, attached to the inlet connection at the bottom of the tank, allows oil to enter the tank when the engine is operating but prevents it from flowing back into the engine sump through the bypass return line after the engine has stopped operating.

a. OIL TEMPERATURE AND PRESSURE. —

Oil temperature and oil pressure, recorded on the engine gage unit (Figure 33, Item 4) on the pilot's upper instrument panel, should be as follows:
Oil Temperature
Recommended . . .75° to 90°C (167° to 194°F)
Emergency . . . . .102°C   (216°F)
Minimum . . . . .60°C   (140°F)
Normal Take-off . . . . .30°C (86°F) minimum
Emergency Take-off . .20°C (68°F) minimum
Oil Pressure
Normal. .65 to 75 psi (desired operating range)
Idling .25 psi minimum

b. OIL COOLER SCOOP CONTROL
(Figure 2, Item 9).

(1) A retractable air scoop for the oil cooler is regulated from the pilot's cockpit by the oil cooler scoop control directly forward of the control stick, under the lower instrument panel. For normal operation, place the control in the "CRUISE" position.

(2) **To open the scoop** (cooling the oil), rotate the control handle clockwise until the indicator registers the desired position.

(3) **To close the scoop** (heating the oil), rotate the control handle counterclockwise.

NOTE

Lock the oil cooler scoop in any desired position by means of a small thumb screw on the left side of the control.

4. OPERATING INSTRUCTIONS.

a. STARTING.

Ignition switch—"OFF."
Mixture control—"IDLE CUT-OFF."
Rotate engine manually—4 or 5 revolutions.
Fuel tank selector—"L.H. MAIN."
Throttle—Set for 600-800 rpm.
Supercharger control—"LOW" blower.
Propeller governor—Take-off rpm (2600 rpm).
Cowl flaps—"OPEN."
Carburetor air—"DIRECT."
Battery and generator switches—On.
Parking brakes—On.
Auxiliary fuel pump—On.
Primer—On (as necessary) (starter up to speed).
Ignition switch—"BOTH" (on).
Starter—Engage.

NOTE

The starter should be engaged as soon as possible after priming.

Mixture control—Advance to "AUTO RICH" as soon as engine fires smoothly; if engine fails to continue running, return to "IDLE CUT-OFF" and repeat starting procedure.

Primer—Operate intermittently, as necessary, until engine runs smoothly.

CAUTION

DO NOT PUMP THROTTLE.

Idle—1000 rpm for 30 seconds. If oil pressure does not register 25 psi within 30 seconds, return mixture control to "IDLE CUT-OFF" and make investigation.

Auxiliary fuel pump—"OFF" when engine is running properly.

NOTE

Allow adequate warm-up before taking off, except in cases of extreme emergency.

VENT LINE

OIL RETURN

OIL TEMPERATURE INDICATOR
OIL PRESSURE GAGE
(ENGINE GAGE UNIT)

ENGINE

FILLER OVERFLOW

OIL TANK

VENT

WARM-UP COMPARTMENT

SUMP

DRAIN PLUG

CHECK VALVE

OIL "IN"
PORT

"Y" DRAIN

OIL "OUT"
PORT

OIL RETURN TO WARM-UP COMPARTMENT

OIL TO ENGINE

OIL COOLER

DRAIN PLUG

TEMPERATURE CONTROL VALVE

LEGEND

Oil Supply
Constant Pressure
Normal Flow of Hot Oil
Normal Flow of Cold Oil
Vent

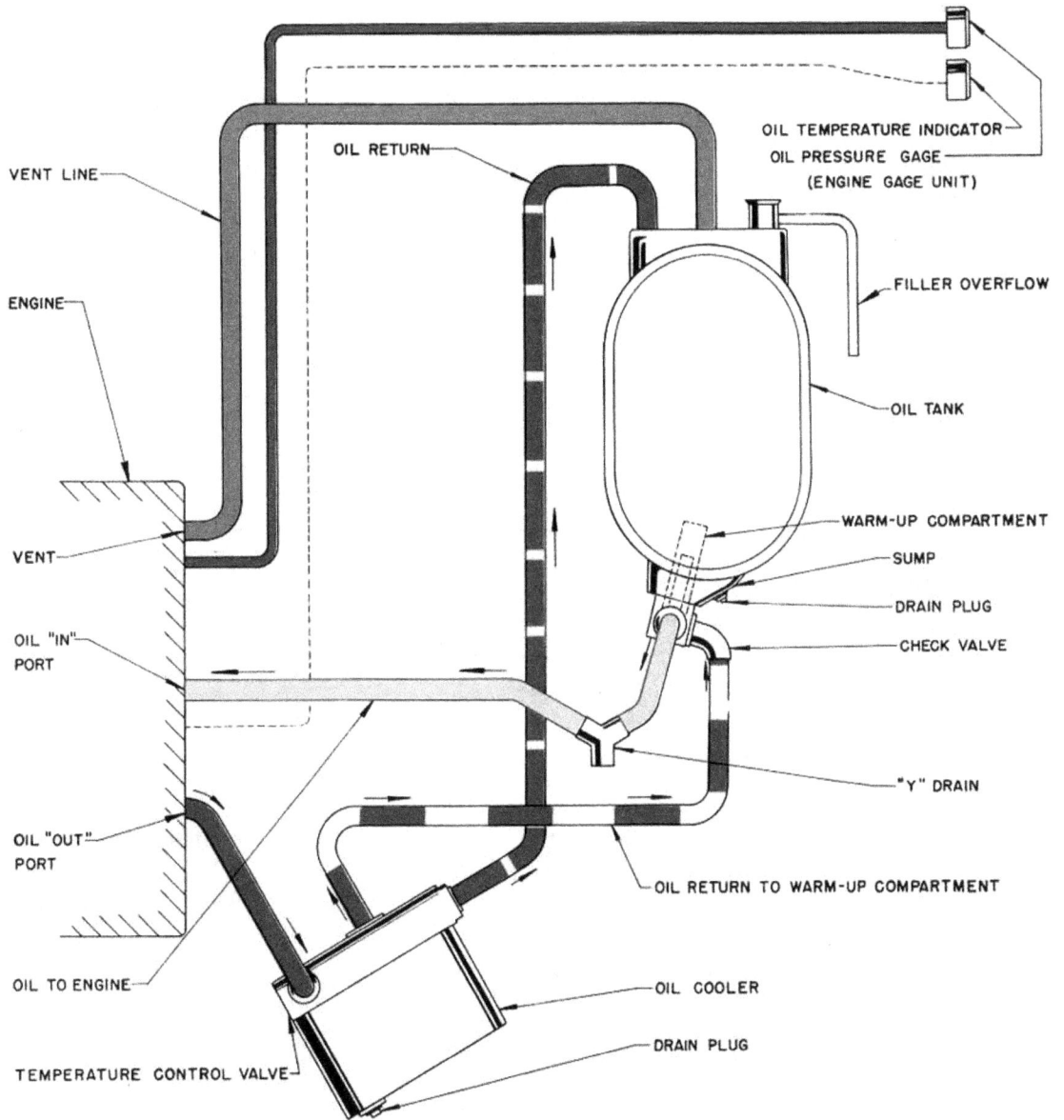

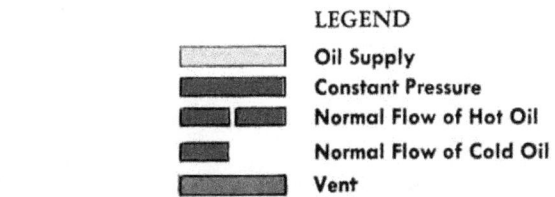

Figure 35—Oil System

b. ENGINE WARM-UP.

Propeller governor control—Take-off rpm (2600 rpm).

Mixture control—"AUTO RICH."

Throttle—1000 to 1200 rpm.

Oil pressure—Watch for fluctuation. If fluctuation occurs, continue warm-up until oil pressure has stabilized.

Oil temperature—Should be at least 30°C (86°F) or in cold weather should rise at least 6°C (11°F) before making following checks.

Manifold pressure—30 in. Hg.

Cylinder head temperature—232°C (450°F) maximum.

Oil pressure—65 to 75 psi. If the oil pressure drops below 65 psi when the throttle is opened, continue the warm-up.

c. ENGINE PERFORMANCE TEST.

(1) PROPELLER AND PROPELLER GOVERNOR CHECK.

(a) Open the throttle to approximately 1700 rpm.

(b) Move the propeller governor control to low rpm (high pitch) setting without moving the throttle.

(c) Observe the tachometer reading. As the propeller increases in blade angle, the engine rpm should automatically decrease.

(d) Move the propeller governor control to the high rpm (low pitch) setting without moving the throttle.

(e) Observe the tachometer reading. If the propeller and propeller governor are operating properly, the original rpm should be resumed.

(2) SUPERCHARGER CHECK.

(a) Open the throttle to 1700 rpm.

(b) Shift rapidly from "LOW" blower to "HIGH" blower.

(c) Open the throttle gradually to approximately 30 inches Hg at sea level.

(d) Observe the manifold pressure when rpm is stabilized.

(e) Shift rapidly from "HIGH" blower to "LOW" blower (do not move the throttle); a sudden decrease in manifold pressure indicates proper operation.

CAUTION

A cylinder head temperature of more than 205°C (401°F) before take-off is not recommended.

(3) MAGNETO CHECK.

(a) Set the propeller governor control to take-off rpm.

(b) Set the throttle at 30 inches Hg.

(c) Move the ignition switch from "BOTH" to "L" and from "BOTH" to "R." Return the switch to "BOTH" between checks to allow the engine to clear out.

(d) Observe the tachometer reading; a drop of 50 rpm to 75 rpm should occur. If a drop of more than 75 rpm is indicated, check for misfiring of one or more cylinders. The check should be made as quickly as possible, since continued running on one magneto will cause the spark plugs to foul.

(4) FUEL PRESSURE CHECK.

(a) Check the engine pump fuel pressure (16 to 18 psi).

(b) Turn the auxiliary fuel pump switch on and check the auxiliary fuel pump pressure; it should be 17.5 to 19.5 psi.

(5) CARBURETOR IDLE MIXTURE CHECK.

(a) Set the throttle to obtain 600 rpm. Move the mixture control lever momentarily (but with a smooth, steady pull) into the "IDLE CUT-OFF" position and observe the tachometer for any change in rpm. A momentary rise indicates too rich a mixture; no change in rpm indicates too lean a mixture.

(b) Return the mixture control to the "AUTO RICH" position before the engine cuts out. Adjust the idle mixture control at the carburetor until a momentary increase of approximately 5 rpm is obtained by means of the above procedure.

(c) Make a final adjustment of the throttle stop on the engine control quadrant in the cockpit to obtain the desired idling rpm with the throttle closed.

d. TAKE-OFF (5 minutes).

Fuel tank selector—"L.H. MAIN."
Auxiliary fuel pump—On.
Cowl flaps—"OPEN."
Carburetor air control—"DIRECT."
Mixture control—"AUTO RICH."
Propeller governor control—Take-off rpm (2600 rpm).
Supercharger control—"LOW" blower.
Throttle—Open to 46.5 inches Hg.
Maximum cylinder temperature—248°C (478°F).

e. MILITARY POWER CLIMB AND LEVEL FLIGHT (2600 rpm—30 min).

Operate the engine according to the "Specific Engine Flight Chart" (Figure 36) and the "Operating Limits Chart" (Figure 37). The throttle and supercharger settings for this condition are given in Table 1, below.

TABLE 1

Altitude (No Ram)	Manifold Pressure Inches Hg.	Supercharger Ratio
S.L.-1,500	46.5	LOW
1,500-9,000	F.T.	LOW
9,000	45.0*	HIGH
12,000	44.5	HIGH
15,000	44.0	HIGH
Above 15,000	F.T.	HIGH

*The altitudes at which these manifold pressures can be obtained vary considerably with carburetor entrance conditions; the above values are for standard air and no ram.

f. RATED POWER CLIMB AND LEVEL FLIGHT (2500 rpm).

Operate the engine according to the "Specific Engine Flight Chart" (Figure 36) and the "Operating Limits Chart" (Figure 37). The throttle and supercharger settings for this condition are given in Table 2, below.

TABLE 2

Altitude (No Ram)	Manifold Pressure Inches Hg.	Supercharger Ratio
S.L.	44.0	LOW
2,700	43.5*	LOW
2,700-12,000	F.T.	LOW
12,000	40.0*	HIGH
15,000	39.5	HIGH
17,500	39.0	HIGH
Above 17,500	F.T.	HIGH

*The altitudes at which these manifold pressures can be obtained vary considerably with carburetor entrance conditions; the above values are for standard air and no ram.

NOTE

If temperature limits are exceeded during a climb, increase the airspeed for cooling.

g. CRUISING.

(1) Conduct cruising operations at any engine power below normal rated power. However, if minimum fuel consumption is of importance, and provided it is tactically feasible, conduct cruising operations in a range not exceeding 65 percent of normal rated power.

(2) Manifold pressure settings and blower shift points for 2200, 2100, and 1700 rpm in the cruising power range are tabulated in the "Power Plant Operation Chart" (Figure 45).

h. DIVING.

Fuel Selector—"L.H. MAIN."

Propeller governor control — 1900 to 2200 rpm.

Maximum diving rpm—3100 (30 sec).

Cowl flaps—"CLOSED."

Carburetor air control—"DIRECT."

Supercharger control—"LOW" blower.

NOTE

This airplane is equipped with a propeller accumulator.

i. STOPPING.

Cowl flaps—"OPEN."

Auxiliary fuel pump—"OFF."

Propeller governor control—Take-off rpm.

Cylinder head temperature—150°C (302°F) or less. If the temperature is higher, allow engine to cool off by idling at 600 to 800 rpm for a short period of time.

Throttle—1000 to 1200 rpm (30 sec).

Mixture control—"IDLE CUT-OFF."

Ignition switch—"OFF" (when engine stops).

Battery and generator switches—"OFF."

Fuel tank selector—"OFF."

THIS PAGE INTENTIONALLY LEFT BLANK.

SECTION III
OPERATION CHARTS AND DATA

1. OPERATING LIMITS CHART (Figure 37).

The "Operating Limits Chart" is used to set operating conditions or to determine engine power at any operating condition within the recommended operating limits of the engine. The section to the left of the chart should be used for "LOW" blower operation and the section to the right for "HIGH" blower operation. Part throttle conditions are those to the left of the oblique heavy-dashed line in both the "LOW" and "HIGH" blower sections; full throttle conditions are to the right of these lines.

a. HIGH POWER—"AUTO LEAN" (Part Throttle).

(1) For a high-power climb, operate along one of the constant-manifold-pressure—rpm lines (sloping lines labeled with manifold pressure and rpm). For a constant rated power climb, use 44.0 inches Hg at sea level; decrease to 43.5 inches Hg at 2500 feet.

(2) Select a level flight condition from a point on one of the designated lines. If an intermediate condition is desired, any manifold-pressure—rpm combination represented in the full throttle portions of the chart can be used for part throttle operation.

b. CRUISING POWER—"AUTO LEAN" (Part Throttle).—

For power conditions below the dot-dash line, the maximum recommended manifold pressures are independent of rpm.

c. HORSEPOWER (any power condition). —

To determine horsepower when the rpm and manifold pressure are known, select the condition in the **full throttle** portion of the section of the chart for the blower ratio in which the engine is operating. Draw a line through the point determined, parallel to the constant-manifold-pressure—rpm lines shown; read the horsepower at the point where this line intersects the pressure altitude line.

d. PRESSURE ALTITUDE. —

Determine the amount of barometric pressure (altimeter window reading) above or below 29.92 inches Hg. Add 100 feet for each 0.1 inch Hg below 29.92 inches Hg; subtract 100 feet for each 0.1 inch Hg above 29.92 inches Hg.

2. CRUISING CONTROL CHART (Figure 40).

The cruising control charts show the engine operating conditions required for cruising at a particular speed, altitude, and weight. Separate charts are provided for the Scout, 500-pound Bomber, and 1000-pound Bomber. After the 500-pound bomb or 1000-pound bomb is released, use the Scout Cruising Control Chart. The charts are used in the following manner:

a. To find the density altitude, proceed vertically from the outside air temperature reading (A) to the pressure altitude line (B).

b. Proceed horizontally to the desired true air speed (C). Note the air-speed indicator reading at (C).

c. Proceed vertically to the base line (D), and follow the guide lines to the gross weight (E).

d. Proceed vertically to the density altitude determined in Step 1. At this point (F), read the rpm and manifold pressure.

e. The following examples illustrate the above procedures:

(1) The following example appears on the 1000-pound Bomber Cruising Control Chart: The airplane is used as a 1000-pound Bomber at a gross weight of 9500 pounds. It is desired to fly at a true air speed of 160 knots at a pressure altitude of 11,000 feet and an outside air temperature of +11 degrees C. Full throttle operation in low blower (47 percent power) at an engine speed of 1980 rpm is required as shown at point (F). The air-speed indicator reading is 128 knots as shown at point (C).

(2) The following examples appear on the 500-pound Bomber Cruising Control Chart: The airplane is used as a 500-pound Bomber at a gross weight of 9500 pounds. It is desired to fly at a true air speed of 160 knots at a pressure altitude of 4000 feet and an outside air temperature of +26 degrees C. A manifold pressure of 29.5 inches and an engine speed of 1840 rpm in low blower (49 percent power) are required as shown at point (F). The air-speed indicator reading is 141 knots as shown at point (C).

(3) The following example appears on the Scout Cruising Control Chart: The airplane is used as a Scout at a gross weight of 9500 pounds. It is desired to fly at a true air speed of 190 knots at a pressure altitude of 18,000 feet and an outside air temperature of −12 degrees C. Full throttle operation in high blower (54 percent power) and an engine speed of 2050 rpm are required as shown at point (F). The air-speed indicator reading is 137 knots as shown at point (C).

SPECIFIC ENGINE FLIGHT CHART

ENGINE MODEL: R-1820-66

AIRPLANE MODEL: SBD-6

Condition	Fuel Pressure Lb/Sq In.	Oil Pressure Lb/Sq In.	Oil Temperature °C
DESIRED	17	70	75-90
MAXIMUM	18	75	102
MINIMUM	16	65	60†
IDLING		25 (min)	

MAX PERMISSIBLE DIVING RPM: 3100 (30 Sec)

Condition	Allowable Oil Consumption*	
NORMAL RATED (Max Cont)	17 U.S. Qt/Hr	28 IMP. Pt/Hr
MAX CRUISE	11 U.S. Qt/Hr	18 IMP. Pt/Hr
MIN SPECIFIC	7 U.S. Qt/Hr	12 IMP. Pt/Hr

OIL GRADE: 1120

FUEL GRADE: 100/130, Spec. AN-F-28

SUPERCHARGER TYPE: Two-Speed

Operating Condition	RPM	Manifold Pressure (Boost)	Horse-power	Critical Altitude With Ram	Critical Altitude No Ram	Blower	Use Low Blower Below:	Mixture Control Position	Fuel Flow‡ (Gal/Hr/Eng.) U.S.	Imp.	Maximum Cyl Temp °C	°F	Maximum Duration (Minutes)
TAKE-OFF	2600	46.5	1300	—	Sea Level	Low	Always use low blower	Auto Rich	154	128	248	478	5
WAR EMERGENCY													
MILITARY	2600 2600	46.5 (FT)** 45-44 (FT)	1300 1000	— —	SL-1500 9000-15000	Low High	9000	Auto Lean††	147 127	123 106	232	450	30
NORMAL RATED (Max Cont)	2500 2500	44-43.5 (FT) 40-39 (FT)	1200 900	— —	SL-2700 12000-17500	Low High	12000	Auto Lean††	130 105	108 88	218	424	Continuous ‡‡
MAXIMUM CRUISE	2200 2200	31.5 (FT) 31 (FT)	760-830 700	— —	SL-9600 17000-20100	Low High	17000	Auto Lean††	63 74	62 53	205	401	Continuous
MINIMUM SPECIFIC CONSUMPTION	1300 1500 1700	31 -29.5 31.5-29.5 32 -29	420 480 540	— — —	SL-4800 SL-6300 SL-7700	Low Low Low	Always use low blower	Auto Lean	29 34 39	24 28 33	205	401	Continuous

*Based on max fuel of 284 U.S. gal (237 Imp. gal) and 16.5 U.S. gal (13.8 Imp. gal) of oil.

†30°C min for normal take-off. 20°C min for emergency take-off.

‡Fuel flows are approximate and will vary with temperature conditions.

**FT denotes full throttle. Critical altitudes given are for standard conditions. Actual critical alt will vary with ram and atmospheric conditions.

††Operation in auto lean is contingent on maintaining head temperatures below limits. Use auto rich when cooling is inadequate in auto lean.

‡‡Engine may be operated for sixty minutes above 218°C (424°F), provided cyl temp are kept below 232°C (450°F).

Figure 36—Specific Engine Flight Chart

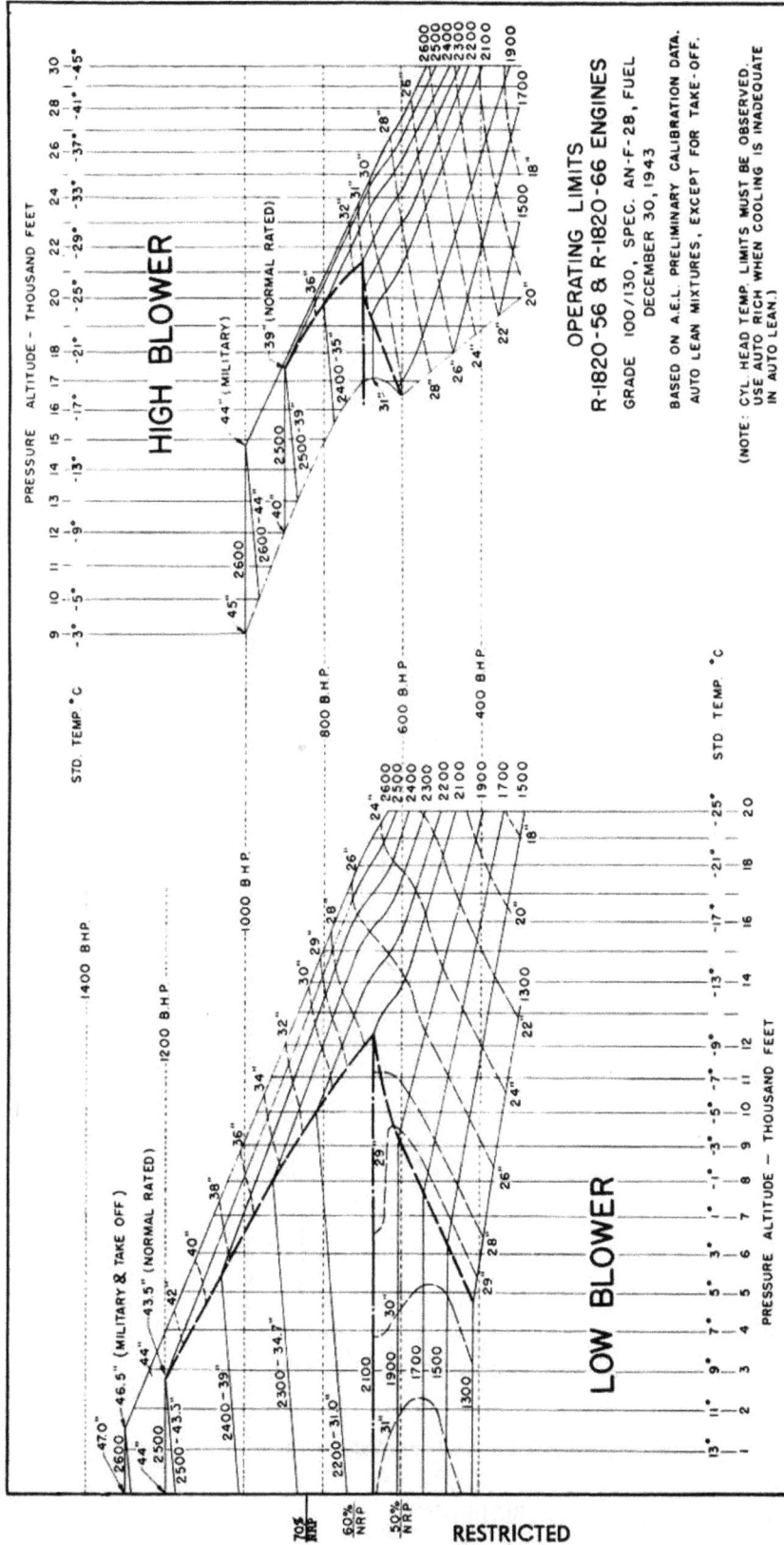

Figure 37—Operating Limits Chart

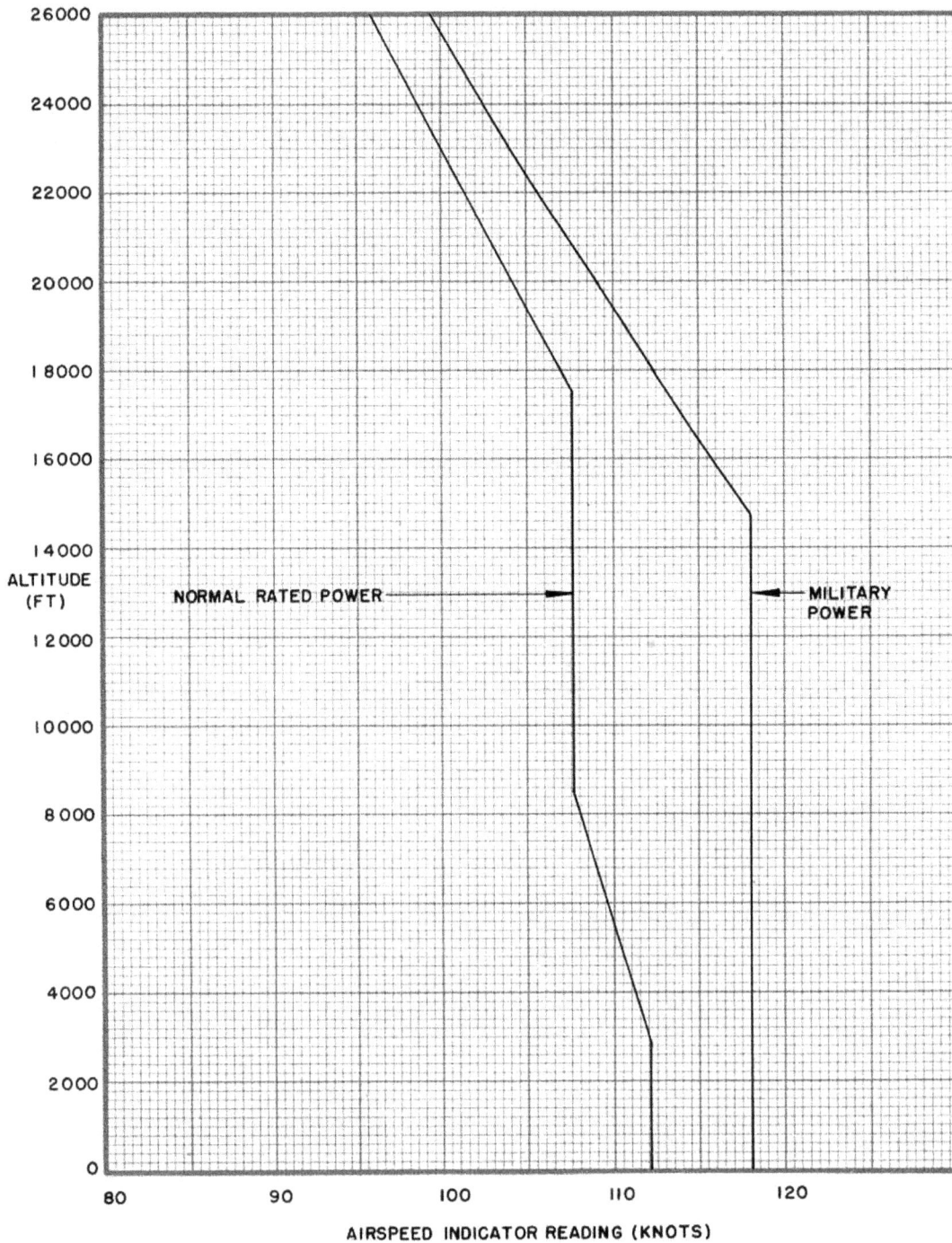

Figure 38—Speed for Maximum Rate of Climb

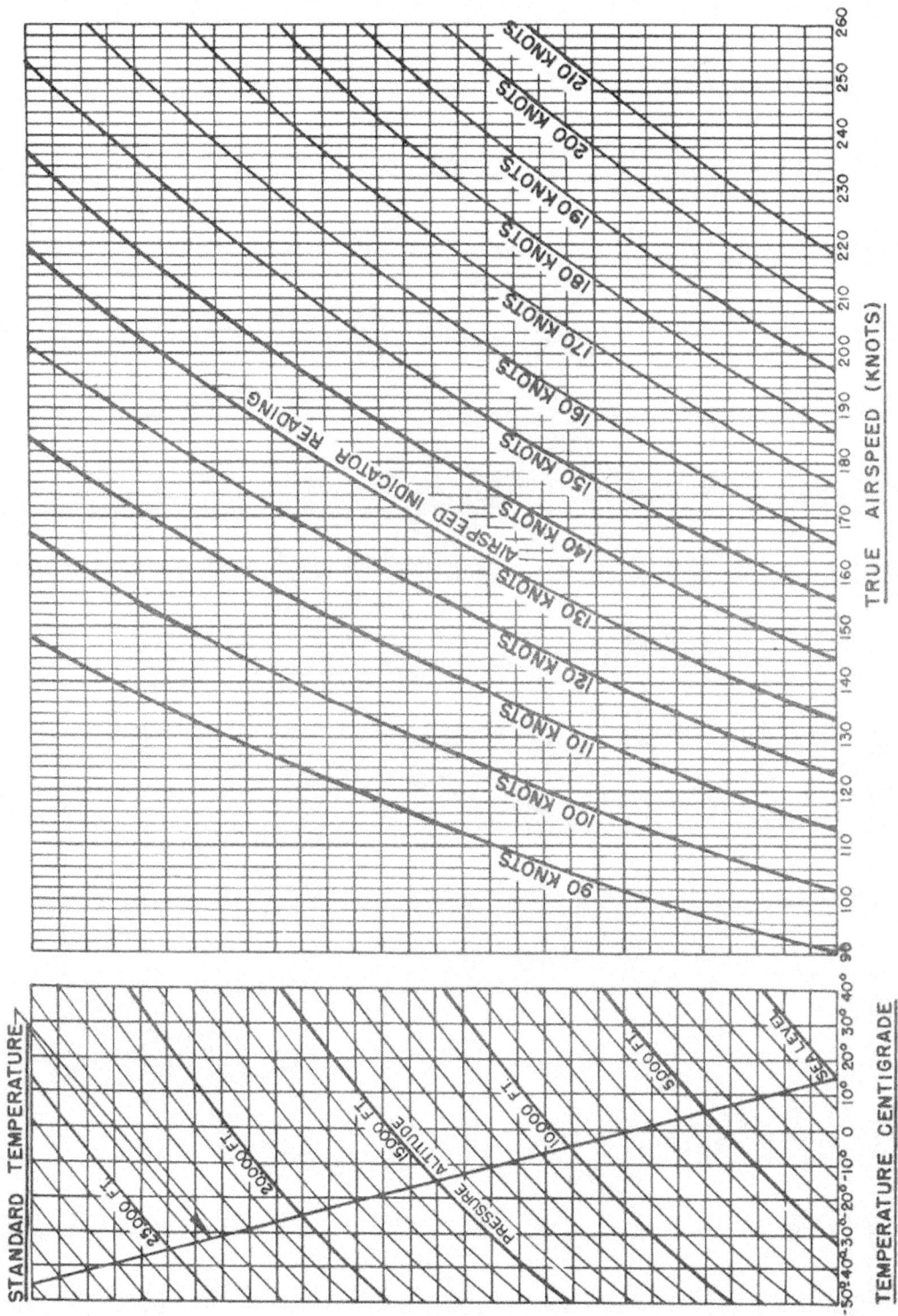

Figure 39—Air-Speed Correction Chart

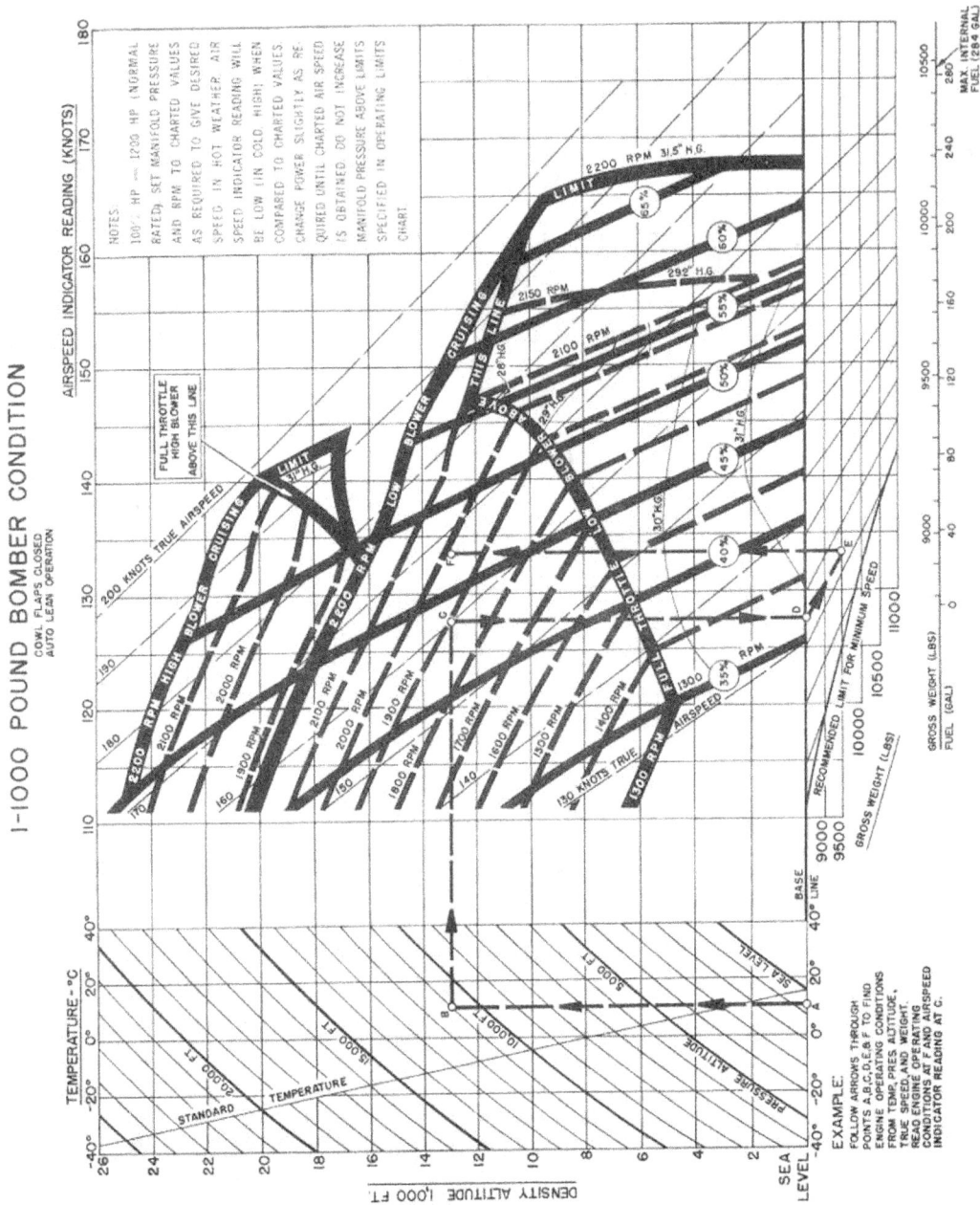

Figure 40—Cruising Control Chart (Sheet 1 of 3 Sheets)

500 POUND BOMBER CONDITION
COWL FLAPS CLOSED
AUTO LEAN OPERATION

Figure 40—Cruising Control Chart (Sheet 2 of 3 Sheets)

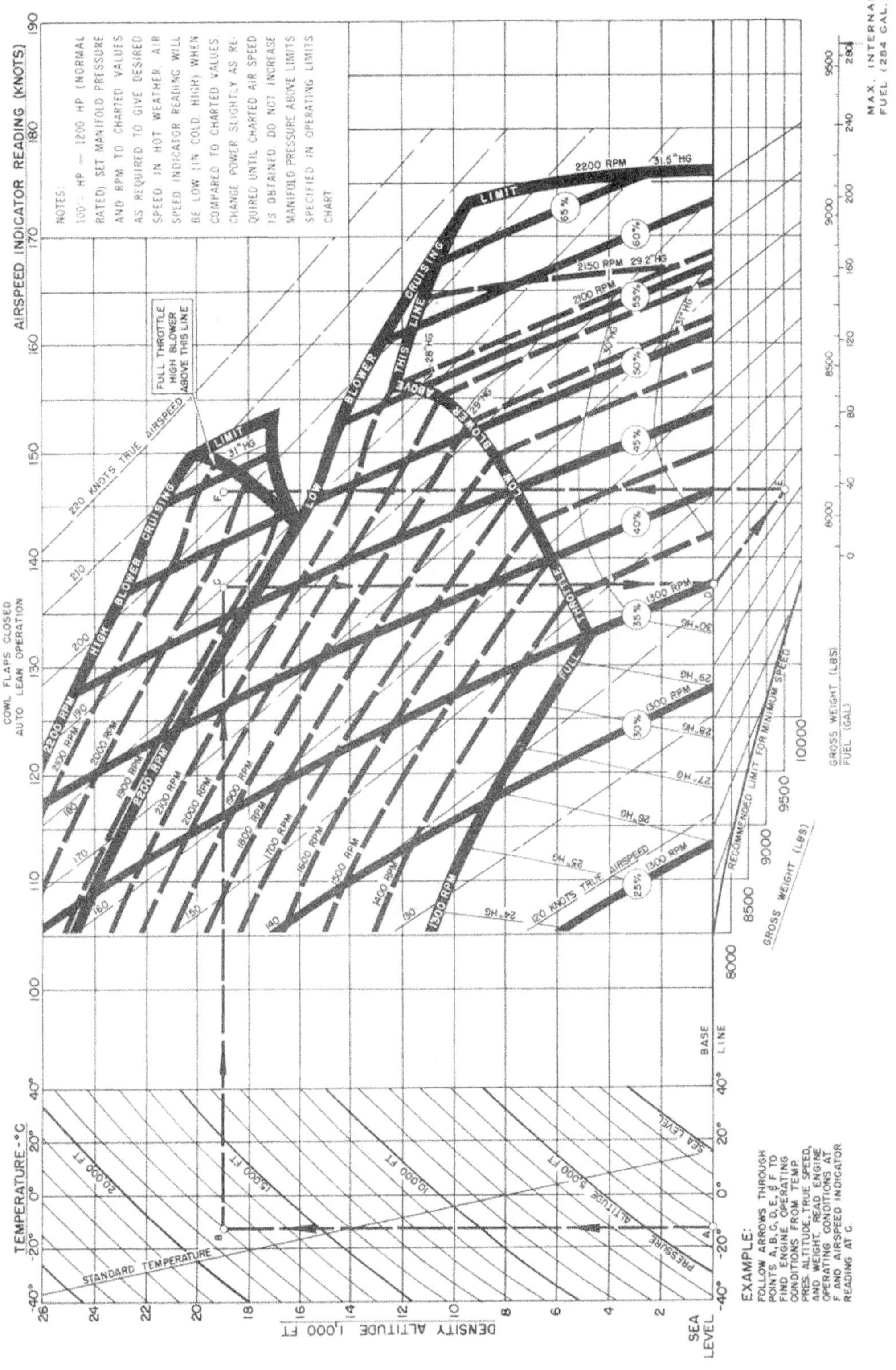

Figure 40—Cruising Control Chart (Sheet 3 of 3 Sheets)

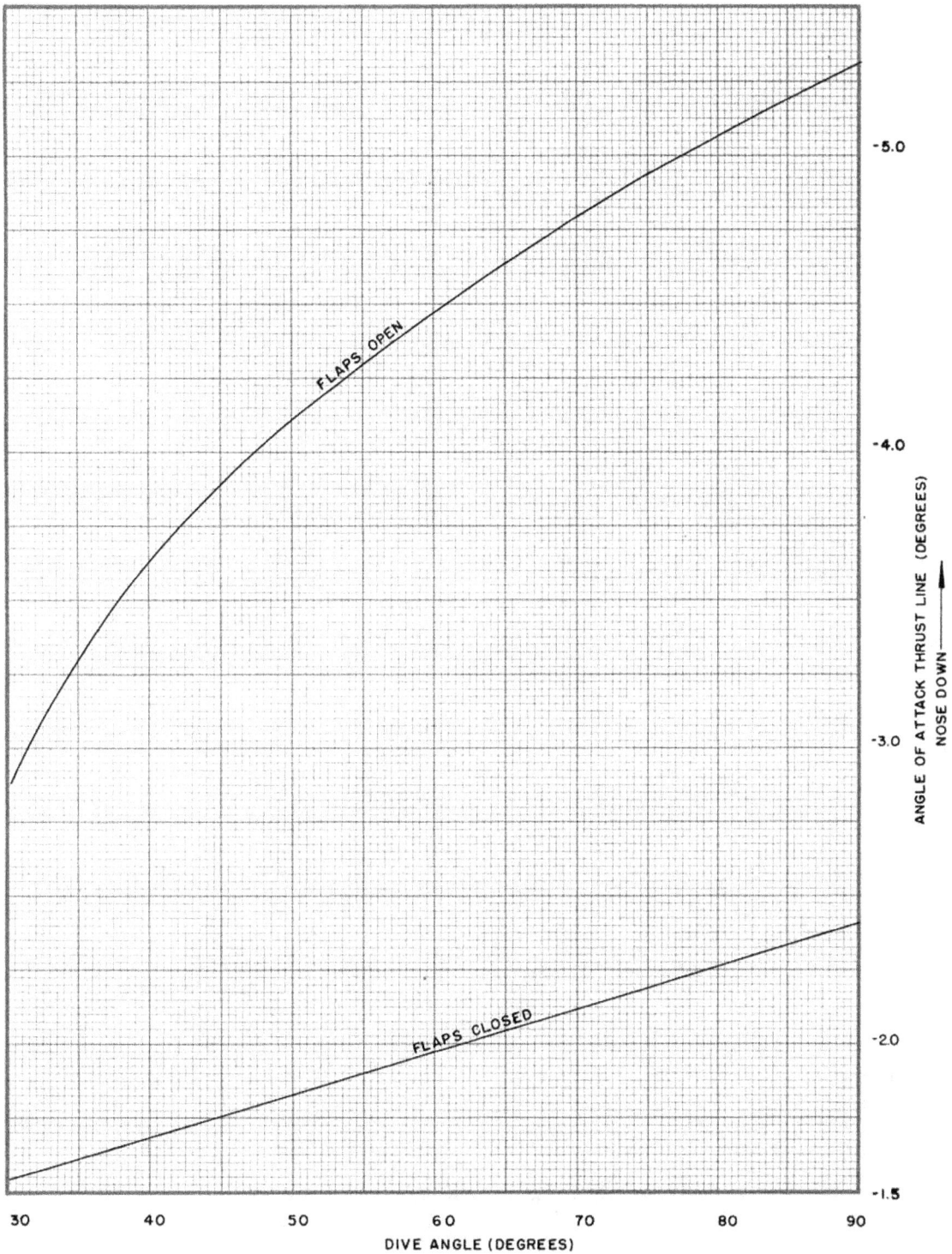

Figure 41—Attitude in Terminal Velocity Dives

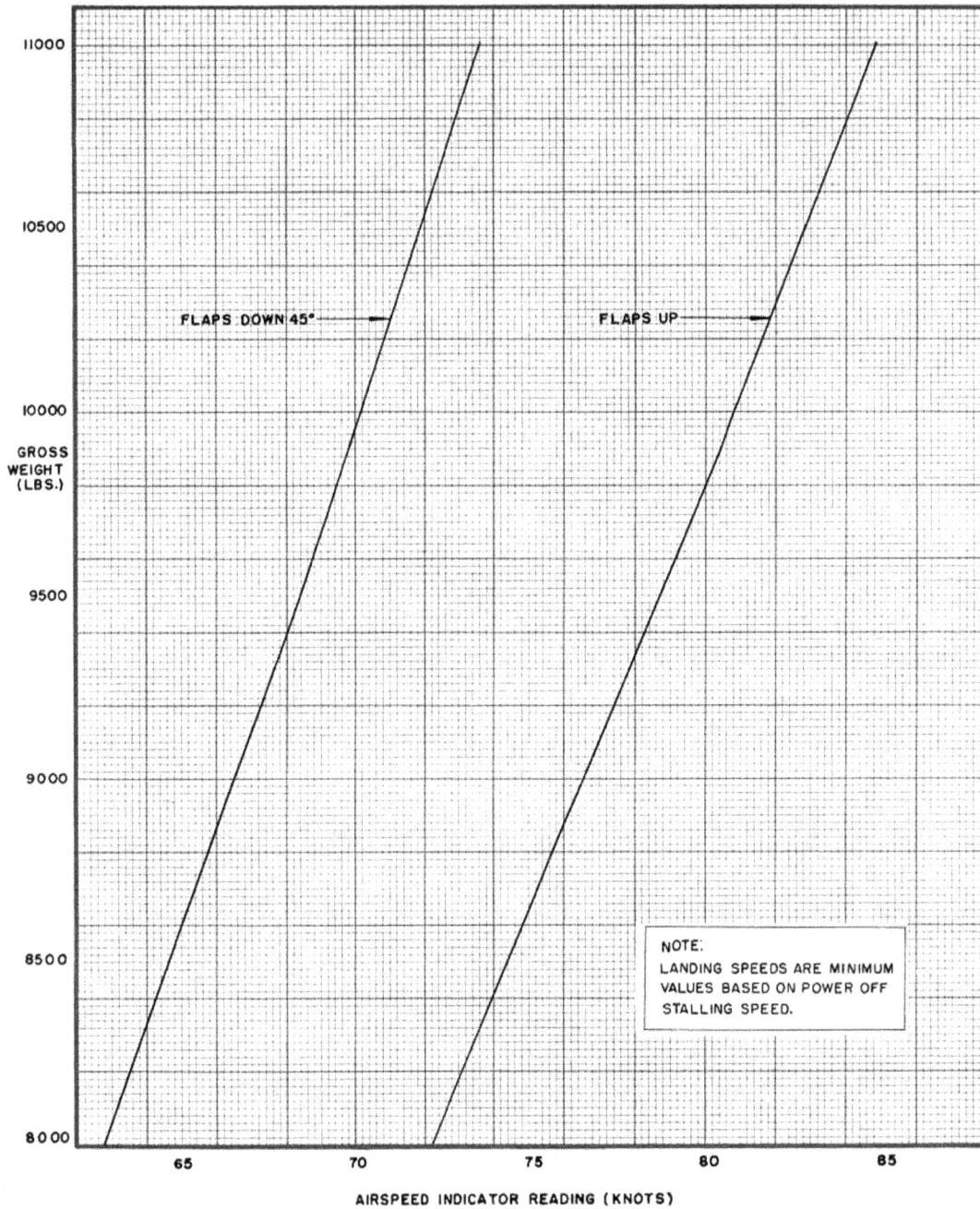

Figure 42—Landing Speed Chart

Gross Weight (In Lbs.)	Head Wind (True Speed in Knots)	At Sea Level	At 2000 Feet	At 4000 Feet	At 6000 Feet	At 8000 Feet
8000	Calm	524	593	684	791	910
	15	316	363	427	502	584
	25	202	237	283	338	401
9000	Calm	680	769	890	1030	1197
	15	423	487	572	673	793
	25	281	329	393	469	561
10000	Calm	865	976	1130	1318	1540
	15	554	635	744	882	1043
	25	378	439	523	629	754
11000	Calm	1080	1219	1420	1659	1952
	15	710	810	956	1137	1355
	25	495	575	689	826	996

NOTE: Take-off distances are minimum values based on take-off speed equal to power-off stalling speed.

Figure 43—Take-off Distances (Ft.)
(Flaps down 45°)

Gross Weight (In Lbs.)	At Sea Level	At 2000 Feet	At 4000 Feet	At 6000 Feet	At 8000 Feet
8000	1272	1350	1432	1522	1620
9000	1430	1520	1611	1713	1821
10000	1590	1688	1790	1903	2022
11000	1750	1858	1970	2095	2225

NOTE: Landing distances are minimum values based on landing speed equal to the power off stalling speed.

Figure 44—Landing Distances (Ft.)
(Flaps down 45°)

	Fuel Press. PSI	Oil Press. PSI	Oil Temp. °C
Desired	17	70	75-90
Maximum	18	75	102
Minimum	16	65	60*
Idling		25 (min)	

Max Diving RPM—3100 (30 Sec)

Military Power			Normal Rated			Operating Conditions	Max Cruise			Cruise			Cruise		
30 Min 232°C			1 Hr. 232°C / None 218°C			Time Limit Hd Temp Lim	No Limit 205°C			No Limit 205°C			No Limit 205°C		
2600 Auto Lean†			2500 Auto Lean†			← RPM → Mix. Control	2200 Auto Lean†			2100 Auto Lean			1700 Auto Lean		
Man. Press.		GPH‡	Man. Press.		GPH‡	Press. Altd. ↓	Man. Press.		GPH‡	Man. Press.		GPH‡	Man. Press.		GPH‡
FT	HIGH BLOWER	62	FT	HIGH BLOWER	56	30000	FT	HIGH BLOWER	39	FT	HIGH BLOWER	34	—	HIGH BLOWER	—
FT		65	FT		57	28000	FT		40	FT		36	—		—
FT		72	FT		63	26000	FT		44	FT		39	—		—
FT		78	FT		73	24000	FT		49	FT		43	—		—
FT		86	FT		83	22000	FT↑		55	FT		48	FT		31
FT		94	FT		93	20000	31.0		62	FT↑		54	FT		33
FT		104	FT↑		101	18000	31.0		58	31.0		58	FT		35
FT↑		116	39.0		104	16000	FT	↕	47	FT	↕	41	FT	↕	30
44.0		125	39.5		104	14000	FT	LOW BLOWER	58	FT↑	LOW BLOWER	45	FT	LOW BLOWER	32
44.5		127	40.0	↕	105	12000	FT		67	28.0		53	FT		34
45.0	↕	125	FT	LOW	96	10000	FT↑		74	28.5		52	FT↑		36
FT	LOW	113	FT		105	8000	31.5		73	29.0		52	29.0		39
FT		124	FT		114	6000	31.5		72	29.0		52	30.0		39
FT		135	FT↑		125	4000	31.5		70	30.0		52	30.5		39
FT↑		145	43.5		130	2000	31.5		67	30.5		52	31.0		39
46.5		147	44.0		130	S. L.	31.5		65	31.0		52	31.5		39

Take-off: 2600 RPM — 46.5 in. Hg — Auto Rich — Direct Air — (5 Min Limit) 248°C Max Head Temp

*30°C min for normal take-off; 20°C min for emergency take-off.

†Operation in auto lean is contingent on maintaining head temperatures below limits.

‡Fuel flows are approximate and vary with temperature conditions.

Symbols: FT—Full throttle.

GPH—Gallons per hour.

↑ —Observe manifold pressure limit until full throttle is reached. (Critical altitudes vary with ram.)

↕ —Shift blower at this altitude. Note that all shifts occur midway between tabulated altitudes.

Figure 46—Power Plant Operation Chart

SECTION IV

AIRPLANE CHARACTERISTICS

1. GENERAL.

The Model SBD-6 Airplane is a single-engined, low-winged monoplane and is designed for dive bombing, smoke laying, or scouting operations. Check-off lists in the pilot's cockpit list the operations which must be completed before take-off, landing, diving, or ground maneuvers. However, it is recommended that the pilot study the information outlined below in addition to the check-off lists. For normal instrument readings, refer to the "Operating Limits Chart" (Figure 37).

NOTE

The flight limitations and restrictions contained in this section are subject to change, and the latest Service instructions and technical orders must be consulted.

2. TAKE-OFF.

a. A load of 200 pounds (passenger or ballast) on the rear seat is advisable, but not essential, to maintain proper balance for take-off and landing.

b. The pilot's cockpit and the gunner's compartment should be checked for any loose gear and for security of ammunition, life raft, and baggage.

c. The pilot may set the control tabs to any deviation from neutral, provided he is thoroughly familiar with the airplane.

d. The airplane retains its normal flying characteristics with either the landing or diving flaps in the closed, partially closed, or fully opened position. However, readjustment of the flight control tabs may be necessary to maintain proper trim at different air speeds. Open the landing flaps to the full "DOWN" position to assist in take-offs from a carrier deck or from a small landing field.

e. The maximum recommended gross weight for catapulting is 11,250 pounds.

3. MANEUVERS.

a. The maximum permissible rpm of the engine during prolonged vertical dives is 3100 rpm (30 seconds). The oil cooler scoop and cowl flaps must be closed during dives, and the supercharger must be placed in "LOW" blower ratio. Prolonged inverted flying is not permissible under any circumstances. Snap rolls with a 1600-pound bomb are prohibited.

b. When external loads are carried, wing-overs and vertical turns are permissible; aileron rolls and inverted flight are permissible only when the airplane is entering dives. When external loads are not carried, the following maneuvers are permissible:

> Loops
>
> Aileron rolls
>
> Snap rolls
>
> Chandelles
>
> One-turn inverted spins
>
> Immelman turns
>
> Wing-overs
>
> Vertical turns
>
> Two-turn spins
>
> Inverted flight (for a few seconds only; must be discontinued before oil pressure drops below 75 psi)

4. LANDING.

a. The use of landing flaps is recommended for all landing operations, since these flaps increase the gliding angle of the airplane and lower the stalling speed. However, fast landings without the use of flaps are permissible on improved airports.

WARNING

The landing gear must be lowered before the landing flaps; otherwise, the landing flaps will be forced up as the landing gear extends.

b. Except when a 1600-pound bomb is being carried, arrested landings can be made with any combination of bomb loadings, provided the fuel load has been reduced to such an extent that the gross weight does not exceed the gross weight of the airplane in the fully loaded scout condition.

c. The indicated landing or stalling air speed of the airplane increases with the weight, but does not increase with the altitude.

d. The airplane can be trimmed in the normal manner for various conditions of flight.

e. The maximum recommended weights for various landing conditions are as follows:

Condition	Gross Weight
Field landing—average fields	8500 lb
Field landing—prepared runways	9000 lb
Arrested landing—average conditions	8350 lb
Arrested landing—controlled conditions	8700 lb

CAUTION

Arrested landings are not permissible while carrying a 1600-pound bomb.

5. SPECIAL PRECAUTIONS.

a. There are no special precautions to be observed regarding the use of this airplane. The only unusual characteristic is that the left wing tends to drop during a stall.

b. Recovery from an involuntary spin can be effected by neutralizing the controls. Various positions of flaps and gear have no effect on the recovery of the airplane from spins.

c. The maximum indicated air speed for diving is 370 knots (425 mph).

d. When a 1600-pound bomb is carried, the following precautions must be observed: The airplane must be restricted to an acceleration of 5.0 g's. To avoid overstressing the bomb displacing gear, no slips, skids, or rolls are permitted at the moment that the bomb is released. The pilot must take added care in flying because a reduction of longitudinal stability has resulted from the center of gravity being moved aft. Arrested landings are not permissible.

e. Catapulting, arrested landings, and landings on average fields are permissible with all bomb loads or with smoke tanks except arrested landings with a 1600-pound bomb. **When filled 58-gallon droppable fuel tanks are being carried on the wing racks, a positive maneuver factor of 5.5 g's shall not be exceeded.**

f. The maximum permissible accelerations under various loading conditions are as follows:

Gross Weight	Permissible Accelerations	
	Positive	Negative
7,500	8.8 g's	4.0 g's
8,000	8.1 g's	3.7 g's
8,500	7.5 g's	3.4 g's
9,000	7.0 g's	3.2 g's
9,500	6.5 g's	3.0 g's
10,000	6.1 g's	2.8 g's
10,500	5.8 g's	2.6 g's
11,000	5.5 g's	2.4 g's
11,500	5.2 g's	2.2 g's

6. TAXIING.

a. All taxiing characteristics are normal and there is no advantage to be gained by lowering the flaps for taxiing in a strong wind. Before starting to taxi, a check should be made to see that the tail wheel is unlocked. To avoid overheating the engine, the cowl flaps should be opened fully. A steady flow of power is recommended in preference to "gunning" the engine.

b. Excessive use of the brakes should be avoided.

c. Visibility directly in front of the airplane is limited; therefore, care should be taken to watch closely for obstacles on the ground.

7. CHECK-OFF LIST FOR TAKE-OFF.

FUEL . . . ."L.H. MAIN"
AUXILIARY FUEL PUMP. . . . . .On
MIXTURE . . . ."AUTO RICH"
SUPERCHARGER . . . ."LOW" blower
PROPELLER . . . . .2600 rpm
COWL FLAPS . . . ."OPEN"
CARBURETOR AIR . . . ."DIRECT"
OIL COOLER SCOOP. . . . ."OPEN"
TRIM TABS . . . . .Check
TAIL WHEEL . . . .(carrier) Unlocked
TAIL WHEEL . . . .(airfield) Locked

8. CHECK-OFF LIST FOR DIVING.

FUEL . . . . .Main tank
MIXTURE . . . ."AUTO RICH"
SUPERCHARGER . . . ."LOW" blower
PROPELLER. . . . . .Maximum cruising (1900-2200 rpm)
COWL FLAPS . . . ."CLOSED"
CARBURETOR AIR . . . ."DIRECT"
OIL COOLER SCOOP. . . . ."CLOSED"
TRIM TABS . . . . .Check
DIVING FLAPS . . . ."OPEN"
     (Do not open flaps in excess of 210 knots)
MAXIMUM RPM . . . . .3100 (30 sec.)
MAXIMUM INDICATED AIR SPEED. . . . . .370 KNOTS (425 mph)

9. CHECK-OFF LIST FOR LANDING.

TAIL WHEEL . . . .(carrier) Unlocked
TAIL WHEEL. . . . .(airfield) Locked
ARRESTING HOOK. . . . .(carrier) "HOOK DOWN"
MIXTURE . . . ."AUTO RICH"
FUEL . . . . .Main tank
AUXILIARY FUEL PUMP . . . . .On
SUPERCHARGER . . . ."LOW" blower
CARBURETOR AIR . . . ."DIRECT"
OIL COOLER SCOOP . . . ."OPEN"
WHEELS (125 knots max.). . . . . .Down
LANDING FLAPS* (110 knots max.). . . . ."DOWN"
    (After flaps are lowered—125 knots max.)
COWL FLAPS . . . ."CLOSED"
    (Check cylinder head temperature)
PROPELLER (approach) . . . . .2200 rpm
TRIM TABS . . . . .Check

  *Wheels must be lowered before landing flaps; otherwise, landing flaps
  will be forced up as landing gear extends.

THIS PAGE INTENTIONALLY LEFT BLANK.

INDEX TO DOUGLAS EL SEGUNDO
PHOTOGRAPH NUMBERS

(Order photographs by photo number only.)

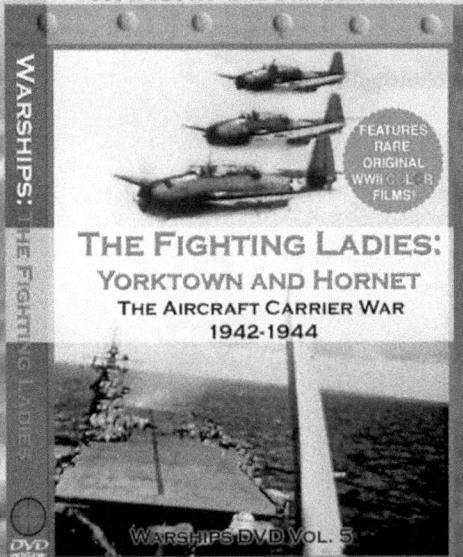

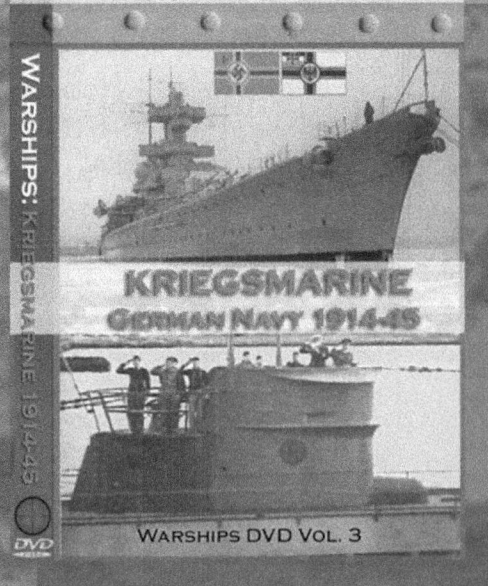

WARSHIPS DVD SERIES

WARSHIPS: PEARL HARBOR TO MIDWAY

PEARL HARBOR TO MIDWAY
THE AIRCRAFT CARRIER WAR
1941-1942

WARSHIPS DVD Vol. 4

DVD VIDEO

HISTORIC U.S. NAVY FILMS
ON DVD!

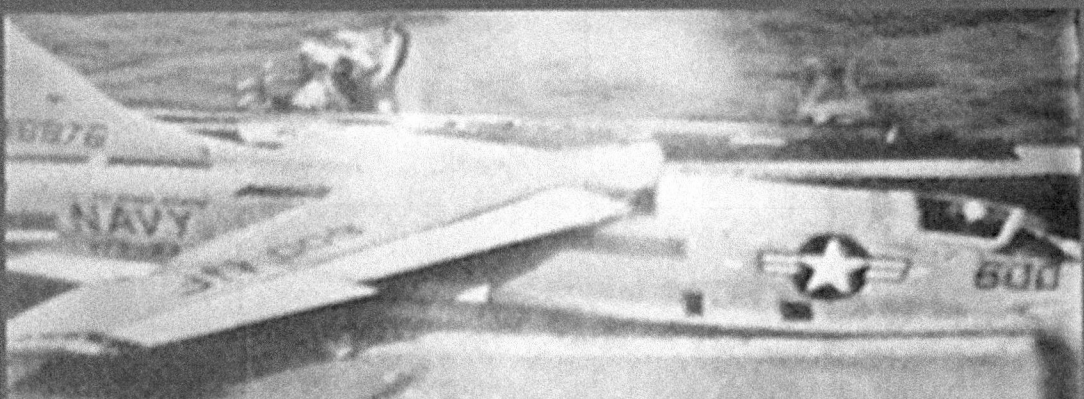

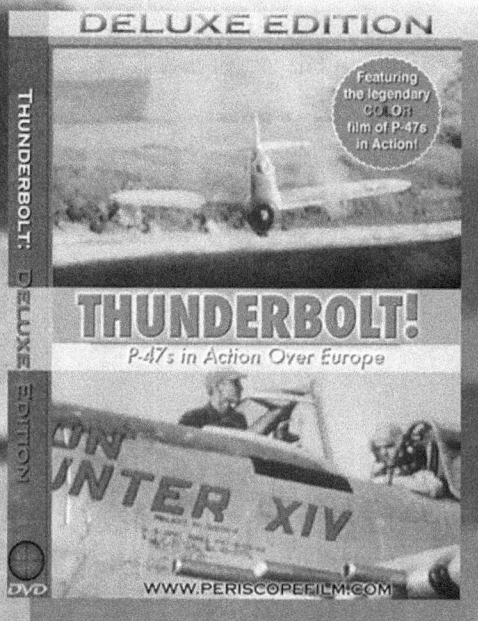

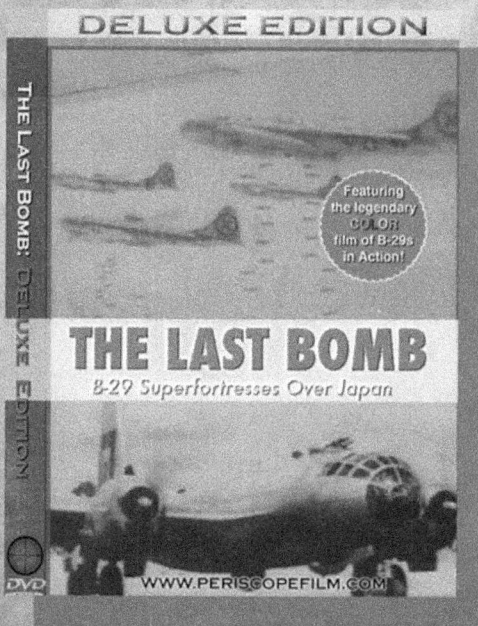

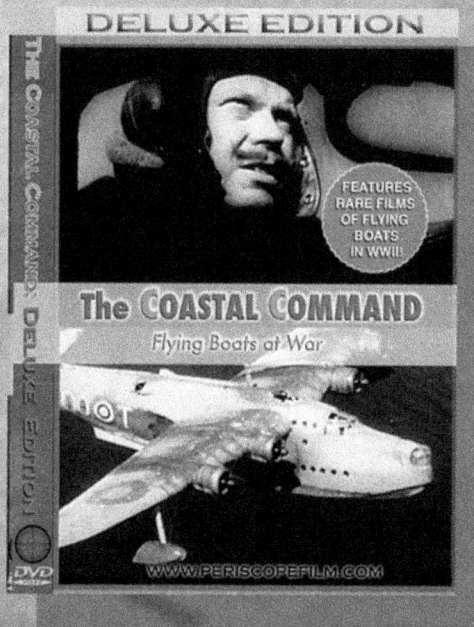

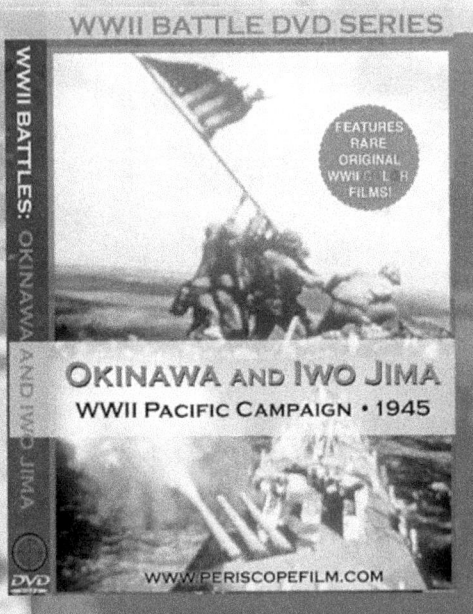

HUGHES XF-11
PILOT'S FLIGHT OPERATING
INSTRUCTIONS

HUGHES XF-11

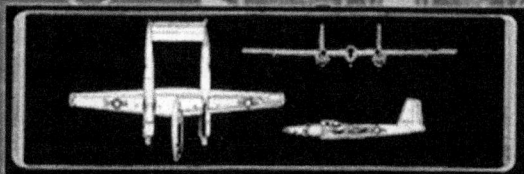

RESTRICTED

Originally Published by the U.S. Army Air Force
Reprinted by Periscope Film LLC

NOW AVAILABLE!

HUGHES FLYING BOAT
MANUAL

SPRUCE GOOSE

RESTRICTED

Originally Published by the War Department
Reprinted by Periscope Film LLC

NOW AVAILABLE!

www.ingramcontent.com/pod-product-compliance
Lightning Source LLC
Chambersburg PA
CBHW062107090426
42741CB00015B/3357